Get HIGH on Vibes in Your Soul's Experiment Called Life!
Playing with Holistic Healing and Metaphysics

VIBRATION EXPERIMENT

LISA DEKEUSTER

BALBOA
PRESS
A DIVISION OF HAY HOUSE

Balboa Press books may be ordered through booksellers or by contacting:

Balboa Press
A Division of Hay House
1663 Liberty Drive
Bloomington, IN 47403
www.balboapress.com
1 (877) 407-4847

The author of this book does not dispense medical advice or prescribe the use of any technique as a form of treatment for physical, emotional, or medical problems without the advice of a physician, either directly or indirectly. The intent of the author is only to offer information of a general nature to help you in your quest for emotional and spiritual well-being. In the event you use any of the information in this book for yourself, which is your constitutional right, the author and the publisher assume no responsibility for your actions.

Print information available on the last page.

ISBN: 978-1-9822-0390-0 (sc)
ISBN: 978-1-9822-0392-4 (hc)
ISBN: 978-1-9822-0391-7 (e)

Library of Congress Control Number: 2018905542

Balboa Press rev. date: 07/11/2018

Contents

The Big Experiment

Everything is going to be okay. Really! For now, that is. Then … it gets *so* much better!

In fact, right here on this earth is as bad as it gets for your soul.

Did you know that you planned this experiment to be a human on this earth on purpose? Yes, you did! You did it for your own soul's learning.

Think of it like going away to college. When you go to college, you leave the comfort of home, live somewhere else, and learn what you can while you're there. Every once in a while you'll visit home, but for the most part, you're chugging away at school.

That means your house isn't your true home—and the earth isn't your true home. Your true home is … wait for it … heaven!

Have you ever felt an emptiness, like something is missing, but you're not quite sure what it is? It's homesickness for your true home of heaven. Our souls, chilling out peacefully and happily at home, had the big idea to come here to the earth to be human beings. We thought it was a great idea. We knew it would be hard, but we knew we would be back in no time flat.

Well, that was when we were thinking about the reality of the infinity of time. When we were born in physical form and started to grow up, we forgot what it was like there. We got all cranky and started moaning and hating.

Don't be a hater.

When your experiment is over and you've learned everything you came for, you'll be safely back in the comforts of home. You'll be so happy to be there again. You'll feel fulfilled and loved. The time you spent here on this earth will seem like just a small fraction of time, and it will soon become only a memory. It will have been worth the work because you'll be happy about all you've learned.

It will feel just like you've made it through the toughest college ever, and you don't have to worry about letter grades in this college! Your final grade will be pass. No matter how you think you're doing here, we're all doing great. It's not easy, and your teachers know that.

It's so perfect at our real home that you probably took on more in this experiment than you wish you had, just like the student who takes more credits at school than he can handle. While he's in the safety and security of home, he's excited to take on a lot, but when he gets there and realizes how hard it is, he feels overworked and kicks himself. The more work he has to do, though, the more he's learning.

The more difficult your life is, the more you're learning and the more courageous you are for sticking around for more. In fact, extreme difficulty most likely indicates that your soul is more advanced because advanced souls often sign up to overcome severe issues. They might choose handicaps, addictions or unexplained depression in order to advance their souls exponentially faster.

During college, science teachers ask tough questions that force you to look more deeply into science for the answer. During this earth experiment, our trials, errors, frustrations and uncertainties are our teachers making life more difficult, making us feel further and further from heaven, and forcing us to look deeper and deeper for the truth. This is what we're here for!

Once you're in school, you shouldn't just drop out voluntarily. If you drop out of this earth experiment early on purpose, it won't be long before your soul regrets it and comes back to try again. Do you really want to start all over again? Your soul really wants to finish this experiment. Wouldn't you rather keep going? Look at how far you've already come!

Think about it— if a bunch of souls got together to plan and volunteer for this big experiment, it was actually very courageous of us to follow through. Not all souls are so brave. Many of our friends stayed put at home where they know they're always going to be happy. That's okay—just like it's okay for those of us on the earth to not go to college here. It's perfectly fine. There's truly no judgment.

If you don't believe any of this, pretend you do while you take a gander through these pages. You can act like it's all fiction and just have fun with it, but the more open you are to it, the more change you'll see in yourself. If you are going to play along, you might want the answer to the following:

What is this big experiment for, anyway? What's the big idea? What's the point?

Drum roll, please …

The point of life on earth is to experience and grow from negativity in order to learn about your spirituality in a place where it doesn't come easily. Sounds about right, right? There is a lot of negativity here, and it sure isn't easy.

At home in heaven, it's easy to have faith because it's right there in front of you and all around you. It's easy to believe you're loved because you can feel it. It's easy to be happy because there aren't any problems! It's easy to believe in our highest power because the love is right in front of you and everywhere and in everything.

Here on our earth, we have to look for hope, faith, love, happiness and divinity. We have to sift through all this negativity to find them.

Where do you seek hope, faith, love, happiness and divinity?

Another drum roll, please …

You can search right there within your own self. You have to slow down your brain to get in touch with your inner knowledge—where your soul is and where you know all the things that are *truly* true.

You can also look to things and people around you, but you have to direct your attention inward to your own soul to know whether to believe what seems to be true.

Have you ever looked for answers in religion and been disappointed? Do you know who made religion? Humans! There are imperfections all over it. The highest of the divine wants all of us to seek within our own souls. There are no imperfections there.

But it's so tough! It really is. Our vibrations here on earth are so heavy with all the things we need to accomplish on a daily basis—working, paying bills, running errands, brushing teeth and more. Then there's the pain and agony of losing loved ones and dealing with loneliness, depression, turmoil and wondering: *What the bleep is the point of life, anyway?*

You need to get in touch with your intuition—where you truly know it all—to raise your consciousness and find your spiritual self and divine nature. Just keep looking!

I'm sorry to tell you that it's not like you stop having problems once you find a bit of the truth. That's because there is so much more wonderful, glorious truth to know. In fact, the more you understand, the more there is for you to learn. However, there is comfort in having the answers you do discover, so life can get easier and easier on your soul as you go.

Some of the lessons our problems teach us are:

- acceptance
- letting go
- patience
- forgiveness
- appreciation
- faith
- overcoming and shedding light into negativity
- love

These are just a small number of lessons we have to learn, but taking things as they come and then letting them go can help you deal with life more smoothly.

I'll remind you now that your courageous soul planned to be here. You also planned how it was going to go for you! Yes, you did—even the stuff you go through that you don't like, even the things about yourself you don't like, and even the people in your life you don't like.

You can call this life plan your chart. It's like a map for your time away from home. You planned it out in a similar way to how high school students plan their college course lists.

As soon as you were born into this world, by divine magic, you forgot how it was going to go. It's all part of the plan to let you learn by experimenting.

Be careful not to judge your journey—you don't even know what the whole thing entails yet. There are various stages of progression of your chart or life journey. Sometimes you may feel a little stuck, like you're getting off track or just not getting ahead.

Guess what? You'll be happy to know that those feelings can be a sign that you are on the right track. A person who's totally off track doesn't bother searching for meaning. Be proud of your accomplishments big and small.

On the other hand, if these feelings become so strong that they turn into depression, it's likely a sign from your soul that you're veering off track. Don't worry! Experiencing this is one of the reasons you're here. It means it's time to do some soul-searching to find out what you need before the stuck energy turns into illness.

You can find your chart, if you really want to, and if you become really good at meditating on it, in the Akashic records. Akashic records are vibrational records of every soul and every human's chart. They can be used as a spiritual resource and as a way of healing whatever might be holding you back.

For now, though, just start with accepting your chart, your life, yourself, the world around you, and others for what and who they are. This will make life flow more freely. Trying to control everything only leads to unnecessary stress.

There are things we can do to accept life's challenges. If we deal with them rather than try to avoid them, we'll be much better off. The trick is to find your center. Your center is the place where you are your true self, deep in your soul. It's who you have always been and who you will always be. It's often hidden under your life situations, personality, work and financial status.

To find your center, sit quietly to get in touch with your true self. It might take a while to find it. Once you have found it, memorize what it feels like to be there. When craziness is going on around you, go to that place within you. You'll realize that acceptance of everything is key and that everything really is okay because you're whole and perfect just as you are—even with all your imperfections. Go back to that place, or to the memory of it, as often as you like. The more often, the better! It's an amazing place to be. Deep down in your soul, you're actually a know-it-all. For real!

Since you're a know-it-all deep down in your soul, don't believe anything I say unless it resonates with you in your soul. Whenever you read or hear something about any given topic, if a little voice inside of you agrees with it, go with that little voice. The trick is hearing that *little* voice.

The big, loud voice of your brain takes over most of the time. The little, quiet voice is in your soul where you hear your intuition. The intuition is like the quiet kid in class who only speaks when spoken to.

Maybe you don't have voices. Most people don't—it's just the phrase that explains something that's difficult to put into words, which is your intuition. You can call it whatever you want—maybe it's just a feeling you get.

Whatever you have going on inside of you, learn it and listen to the soul part. Your truth resides deep within you—even more than it does in your brain.

I'm just a researcher and truth seeker sharing ideas that resonate with me, but I can tell you one thing for sure—even though life on earth wasn't meant to be super easy, it also wasn't meant to be so darn hard! The heaviness that weighs in our hearts, minds and energy centers makes life tough and buries our intuition, causing our energy vibrations to flow more slowly.

Just following your intuition is enough to make your vibrations flow more easily again.

Dig within your soul and you'll shake up those high vibes!

Playtime for the Kid in You

Playtime sections include activities for the kid in you to practice soul-expansion habits. You can do them alone or get a friend of any age to tag along in your games.

Also, you can do them on paper or in your head no matter what the "instructions" say. I put the word *instructions* in quotes because they're not hard-and-fast rules. You should follow them in the way that works best for you—whatever that means.

Also, it's great to have time to play, but the best time to take short breaks for playtime is when you think you have the least time for it. The busier you are, the more overwhelmed you feel, and the more you need the clarity that these short activities will bring you.

Most importantly—have fun!

Experiment with Experiences

How do you feel when you're in a horrible situation and someone says, "It'll be okay"? Does it make you feel better? Or do you feel like they're lying?

_____

_____

Would it make you feel better if you were 100 percent sure that it really was going to be okay?

_____

_____

Do you believe this life is a big experiment for our souls? Why or why not?

_____

_____

If life is a big experiment for our souls, how courageous do you think a soul is to be part of this experiment?

_____

_____

Can you think of more lessons people have to experience on earth?

_____

_____

_____

If You Could Change Your Chart

Imagine you could write your chart right now for the rest of your life. Fill in the age you are now and continue from there:

Age _____

In the next five years, these are the situations that will happen in my life:

_____

_____

_____

These are the lessons I will have to learn:

_____

_____

_____

These are the struggles I'll have in order to learn those lessons:

_____

_____

_____

People who will be there to help me:

_____

_____

What I will be like as a person:

_____

_____

_____

In the next twenty-five years, these are the situations that will happen in my life:

_____

_____

_____

These are the lessons I will have to learn:

_____

_____

_____

These are the struggles I'll have in order to learn those lessons:

_____

_____

_____

People who will be there to help me:

_____

_____

What I will be like as a person:

_____

_____

_____

Who's Going to Accept *That*?

Choose one of the following situations and circle it.

- You wake up late and your car won't start.
- You lose your phone and can't get a new one until next week.
- You had plans with a friend who canceled on you, but you still want to go to the shindig.

Draw a comic strip—with one scene on each segment—where you try to control the outcome. Make sure you include the actual outcome. Try to make it realistic.

_____ _____ _____ _____ _____

Draw a second comic strip where you accept what has happened without trying to control the outcome. Make sure you include the actual outcome. Try to make it realistic.

_____ _____ _____ _____ _____

Intuit *This*!

Make a game of listening to types of feelings.

List a decision you have to make:

_____

_____

Write down one feeling you have about this decision:

_____

_____

Write down another feeling you have about it. For example, what would happen if you were to make the opposite decision?

_____

_____

Write the choice you've made:

_____

_____

Later, come back and answer this: How did it turn out?

_____

_____

Do the same with feelings you have for another decision you need to make.

A decision you have to make:

_____

_____

One feeling you have about this decision:

_____

_____

Another feeling you have about it. For example, what would happen if you were to make the opposite decision?

_____

_____

Write the choice you've made:

_____

_____

Later, come back and answer this: How did it turn out?

_____

_____

Which feeling tends to work out best for you?

_____

_____

Whatever it is, this is likely the way your intuition speaks to you. Keep listening and trusting!

Scientifically Speaking

What in the world is real? How do you know? Spirituality might seem like hogwash to some scientific minds. A lot of it might even seem fluffy for spiritual people with analytical minds. However, scientists continue to put forth more and more evidence to support spirituality—from the miniscule to the overwhelming. Scientific proof can offer explanations for what we feel is true within ourselves.

When intuitive feelings aren't backed by proof, they are easier to doubt. Yes, blind faith is wonderful, but real proof goes a long way, too! When we're trying to determine what is real and what is not, we have to realize the outside world and the world of the mind are two totally separate things that intermingle and determine how our brains process thoughts.

The outside world is made of matter; it is what we often think of as being reality. The world of the mind is made up of conscious and unconscious experiences. Your personal perceptions of what you see and hear, your emotions and your memory all leave gaps. So, the mind fills in the gaps … and usually gets it wrong. Who knows what we'll stew up as real?

Hello, illusions!

These worlds come together in very mysterious ways, causing us to interpret and misinterpret more than we could ever know because a lot is happening in the unconscious that, by definition, we're not even aware of. In fact, you could define the word *unconscious* as the part of your mind that affects your thoughts while being inaccessible to the conscious mind.

The unconscious mind deals with your basic necessities for survival and life functions, while the conscious mind can be thought of as optional. There are animals that survive with seemingly no consciousness, but they have many unconscious natural instincts. The conscious mind can't possibly process everything that happens around you. Scientists say that we're only conscious of about 5 percent of our cognitive function!

It's been found that if two unmoving images are shown to us, with only one in each eye, we'll only perceive one of them—it won't be a superimposed version of the two as you might think. After a while, you'll perceive the other image, but not the first one. It'll just keep alternating. Crazy, huh? If, instead of two still images, one is moving, your brain will only perceive the action-packed image and not the one that's remaining still.

Science also proves that our memories are way worse than we realize. Studies have shown multiple people with supposedly great memories recalling the same situations quite differently—only to be shown through recordings from the time being recalled that all were actually getting it quite wrong.

On top of that, it's been proven that people often believe their feelings came from one specific instance when they actually came from another. For example, say someone makes you mad and you go talk to someone else about it. You probably won't even realize it, but in the future, you'll associate the second person with the negative emotion and begin to have negative feelings toward that person. If that's not a good reason to avoid asking people for gossip, what is? Do you want people unconsciously associating you with those negative emotions?

When you hear gossip, even if you use your conscious mind to overlook someone's opinion, your unconscious is influenced in unpredictable ways. It's important to let your conscious mind take over and not be negatively influenced more than necessary. And don't ever gossip in front of kids! Even if you tell them not to repeat it, they will be influenced by what you say. Their opinions will change—and so will the way they treat the person being talked about.

The unconscious mind is why ads work so well. Even if you don't want to be fooled by the wit of advertising committees, their messages will sink into your brain. The more you become aware of this, the easier it will be to pass it off as simply good advertising rather than falling for buying something you don't even really want.

All different characteristics—color, font, tone, and texture—influence whether you want to read a book or buy certain products. To more of an extreme, an unattractive font makes instructions more difficult to follow, but a font you like makes the same instructions easier to follow. A cereal box with a picture of a celebrity or animal you like is more delicious than the same cereal from a plain box if your unconscious mind is taking over, which is most of the time.

Researchers gave a group of people computer lessons. The only difference between the lessons was that one had a female voice and the other male. While participants were using their conscious minds to think about the meanings of the words, their unconscious minds were evidently judging the speaker by voice and gender. The female's voice earned higher ratings on topics about love and relationships, while the male's voice earned higher ratings on the more dominant topics.

It's really difficult to say how much of your conscious or unconscious is responsible for your feelings and actions because you're constantly shifting back and forth between them. With practice, you can train yourself to bring more of the unconscious to the conscious and influence it according to how you want to live your life.

You can think of your unconscious as the invisible part of your brain that's constantly receiving subliminal messages. It influences your conscious experience in so many ways, including how you view yourself, how you view other people, how you judge situations, the significance you place on outside events, how you make decisions, and all the actions you take because of instinct. That's a big job for a part of the brain that some people don't even know exists!

Is it scary to think there's a whole lot more happening in your mind than you even know about? Our constant misperception of reality adds mental stress to life. Mental stress leads to physical effects, and both affect us spiritually.

Because we experience the world so indirectly and have so many misperceptions of the conscious and unconscious minds interweaving, modern neuroscience teaches us to consider all our perceptions as illusions. That makes me feel like I'm living in a movie where only the viewer realizes what's actually going on—if that!

All of these illusions can make life full of uncertainty, but if you think about it a different way, you realize you really can conjure up any reality you want to within yourself.

Why not have fun with it? You decide! How positive are you?

How negative are you? Did you know that an average of 70 percent of thoughts are negative? Yikes! Doesn't that sound miserable? It's natural to be negative since humans were wired to prepare for the worst in order to make sure we have what we need while we're hunting in the wild and stuff. Since it's not necessary in the modern world, the negativity is more often destructive rather than productive. Negativity makes the brain think there's an immediate threat, which causes the fight-or-flight instinct to kick in and makes it difficult to handle actual day-to-day situations.

Do you like to be around negative people? Do you like to be around mean people? Probably not, but are you mean to yourself? Are you your own worst critic? Think about the way you talk to yourself and then decide not to hang around negativity from others or from yourself.

Self-talk is important because you're listening! What you tell yourself weighs on your mind even more than when other people talk down to you. It makes sense since you can't get away from yourself no matter how hard you try.

Since your self-talk is so powerful, you might as well make it good. Start by paying close attention to the way you talk to yourself in your head. Change whatever you need to make life more fun. Self-talk doesn't just apply to opinions about yourself. It also applies to things going on in your life. If you say things to yourself like, "I have to do the dishes," for example, you're putting a negative vibe on doing your dishes, and that tells your brain that it's a bummer. Simply change it to, "I'm going to do the dishes," or if you can convince yourself that you like to do dishes because you get to take time for your imagination to wander while you do your chore, say, "I *get* to do the dishes." Instead of thinking of cleaning up the kitchen after dinner as a chore, remind yourself that you'll be happy to have an organized kitchen when you wake up for breakfast.

When I started a new job, I stopped the first coworker I met from giving me her scoop on our other coworkers because I wanted to see things through rose-colored glasses. I enjoyed my first couple years there a lot more than I did once I started letting people tell me their opinions! That's because my inner voice had different thoughts about them.

If you'd like to do some scientific pondering about the effects of changing the words of your inner voice, think about how the placebo effect works. If you have a headache and take pain medicine, your pain goes away. If you have a headache and take a placebo, your pain goes away.

It's all about what your brain thinks is going on. So, let your brain think the best!

Where thoughts go, energy goes. Setting intentions is the starting point of your creative powers. Some psychologists say there are two ways to get to the truth. You could be like a scientist gathering observations and proving theories or you could be like a lawyer who begins with the desired conclusion and seeks evidence to support it. Which one sounds like a more reasonable way to approach life? You might want to be better at the scientist part of you, but most people are way better at convincing themselves of whatever they want to believe.

Have you ever noticed how after a team wins, fans talk about how great the team played, but after a loss they talk about bad luck? That's okay! Don't count us all as fools. Studies also show that people with the most accurate views of themselves tend to be moderately depressed and have lower self-esteem. That is sad, but it helps prove that positivity about yourself is good for your survival.

Connect four! Science, metaphysics, holistic healing and play all tie together …

Science deals with the conscious and unconscious through facts that can be seen through studies and research.

Metaphysics deals with the conscious and unconscious through seemingly more abstract findings, but that doesn't make those findings untrue. The proof is in the science of it more and more as time goes on.

It wasn't that long ago that holistic healing methods like acupuncture and chiropractic care were talked about like they were completely unnatural, and yoga was seen as being like a religion. The more you discover and play with the science, metaphysics, and holistic healing methods presented here, the more you'll see how they all tie together! As for the mysteries left unanswered, that's where your spiritual journey continues.

Playtime!
Speaking Scientifically

Can you think of times you should let your conscious mind take over and times you should listen to your unconscious? If so, jot them down here:

Times to let the conscious mind take over the unconscious mind:

_____

_____

_____

_____

_____

_____

Times to let the unconscious mind take over the conscious mind:

_____

_____

_____

_____

_____

_____

-Or-

Write down one opinion that you have about someone you know:

_____

Do you think this opinion came from your conscious mind or your unconscious mind?

_____

Write down the basis for your opinion:

_____

_____

Now that you've thought about the basis for your opinion, do you think you should change your answer about where the opinion came from in your mind?

_____

_____

_____

_____

-Or-

Experiment to see how people perceive you and treat you differently depending on the way you look. Pick a very different type of fashion than you're used to and go to a public place like a festival or a mall. If you usually wear a T-shirt and tennis shoes, maybe you should dress up in fancy clothes. If you're usually in a suit and tie or dress, wear a T-shirt or white tank top. You could grow a beard, wear funny glasses, do your hair in a completely different way, or use a wheelchair. It would be even more fun to go out looking like a complete slob. Drool a little. These might be eye-opening experiences!

-Or-

Talk to strangers (if you're an adult). Find chances to have light-hearted conversations with people you meet. People you have never met can help you see the world in a different way and break the stagnant thought patterns you experience on a daily basis.

-Or-

Put on magic glasses to see the world through rose-colored glasses.

-Or-

Contemplate the collective unconscious, which is the unconscious set of beliefs that all people of a certain group hold. What would you like to change?

Tying It All Together

Do some research in the metaphysics and science sections of your local bookstore or library. Find ways they agree and ways they disagree.

Notice the dates that books were published so you can note changes in the ways of thinking. You'll see how science eventually comes around to metaphysical findings.

Chakras and Auras

Spinning inside of you, shooting off from you, and all around you is energy.

The highest levels of vibration in your body are your chakras. There are hundreds of them. We'll go into detail on each one. Just kidding. There *are* hundreds of them, but we'll just go into detail on the main seven.

The main chakras involve your legs, sacral area, solar plexus, heart, throat, brow and crown. Think of chakras as subtle energy bodies or wheels of energy or light. This energy is also called prana, chi, vital bodies or life force energy.

How do we even know chakras exist? Actually, many people discovered chakras at different times by paying attention to the mind and body connection. They could feel sensations in certain parts of their bodies while seeing certain colors in their mind's eye. When someone discovered it was the same color for each person depending on which part of the body it was, they began to make connections.

The coolest connection, in my opinion, is that we are the same color as the rainbow! We're red at the root, orange at the sacral area, yellow at the solar plexus, green at the heart, blue at the throat, indigo at the brow and violet at the crown. Just call yourself Roy G. Biv. You're also the same color crystals give off in the sunlight. It's mighty fine how the universe works, isn't it?

More and more connections have been made, including that each chakra affects certain endocrine glands, which affects certain bodily functions and emotions. The chakras connect to specific elements, and there are physical movements including yoga poses that can help you open them. Certain mantras and hand positions can help you focus on the health of the particular chakra.

Root Chakra

Color: Red
Location: Base of the spine, legs, bones, and teeth
Element: Earth

Helps you feel: Grounded, aligned, safe, vital, ambitious, and secure with food, shelter and the basic necessities for life
Activities: Walking around barefoot, dancing
Yoga poses: Triangle pose, single leg/hip lifts
Positive thought: I have, I own, I deserve to have, I attend to my mind, body and spirit
Sound: Lam
Hand position: Connect pinkie and thumb with the other fingers out
Blocked by: Fear
Blockages show up through: Worries about finances or stability, fatigue, nervousness, restless leg syndrome or feeling disconnected from the world

Sacral Chakra

Color: Orange
Location: Pelvic bowl, reproductive organs, bladder, kidneys, colon, sacrum and bodily fluids
Element: Water
Helps you feel: Passionate, sexual, and creative, including creativity with music, poetry, dream manifestation and physical enjoyment
Activities: Take a candlelit bath or watch a romantic movie
Yoga poses: Extended side angle, supported bridge
Positive thought: I feel, I am emotionally balanced, I respond rather than react so that I make wise choices, and I bring my best self forward
Sound: Vam or vwam
Hand position: Connect ring finger and thumb with the other fingers out
Blocked by: Guilt and humiliation
Blockages show up through: Control issues, PMS, prostate problems, sciatica, lower backache and bowel dysfunction

Solar Plexus Chakra

Color: Yellow
Location: Upper abdomen, stomach organs, liver, pancreas, upper intestines
Element: Fire

Helps you feel: Personal willpower, strength to survive, purposeful, confident, understood, assertive and responsible for the self

Activities: Spend time in sunshine or with close friends

Yoga poses: Side plank, side hip lifts

Positive thought: I act, I do, I accept myself as I am, and I have deep compassion and understanding for myself

Sound: Ram

Hand position: Connect middle finger and thumb with the other fingers out

Blocked by: Shame, anger

Blockages show up through: Feelings of rejection, low self-esteem, and hope for others to supply your needs

Heart Chakra

Color: Green

Location: Center of chest and circulation of the lungs

Element: Air

Helps you feel: Compassion, unconditional love, emotions, joy, respect, surrender, and expressive of feelings to others as well as to the self

Activities: Eat green foods or partake in any enjoyable solitary hobby to connect to self

Yoga poses: Upward facing dog (cobra), blooming flower

Positive thought: I radiate light and live as freely as the shining, radiant sun; I balance

Sound: Yam

Hand position: Connect pointer finger and thumb with the other fingers out

Blocked by: Grief

Blockages show up through: Heart problems, lack of compassion, fear of rejection, feelings of loving too much, and being skeptical of those who want to love you

(The heart is the central chakra, so it connects the other chakras together.)

Throat Chakra

Color: Blue

Location: Neck, throat, thyroid, mouth, teeth, tongue, jaw

Element: Ether or space

Helps you feel: In control of speech and able to clearly and successfully express oneself in an honest and confident manner without judgment

Activities: Sing, be straightforward and honest

Yoga poses: Downward dog, camel (knee stand with backbend, hands to feet)

Positive thought: I speak, and I express myself freely and appropriately

Sound: Ham

Hand position: Thumb placed in palm with the fingers out

Blocked by: Lies

Blockages show up through: Inability to express what you want, inability to realize your dreams, neck pain, headaches and hoarseness in throat

Brow Chakra or Third Eye

Color: Indigo

Location: Middle of forehead or between the eyebrows, skull, eyes, brain, nervous system and senses

Element: Universe, universal life energy

Helps you feel: Intuitive, wise, clairvoyant, and connected to your senses, your true self, your higher consciousness, and the true nature of life while strengthening visualization

Activities: Reward yourself with praise when you succeed intuitively and be more attentive when you're with others

Yoga poses: Child's pose, cat/cow

Positive thought: I see, and I am wise about my priorities and intuition

Sound: Om

Hand position: Open hands with palms up

Blocked by: Illusion

Blockages show up through: Lack of inner guidance, insomnia and paranoia

Crown Chakra

Color: Violet, pure white light or both

Location: On the top of the head, spinal cord, brain and nerves

Element: Universe

Helps you feel: Connected to the divine energy of the universe and the wisdom and unity of it

Activities: Watch an inspirational movie or read an inspirational book

Yoga poses: Rabbit, rolling on crown of the head, side head lifts

Positive thought: I know, I trust, and I connect with a natural knowledge of how to proceed

Sound: Silent Om (feel the vibrations and energy in the universe)

Hand position: Open hands, palms up

Blocked by: Ego and attachment

Blockages show up through: Living in fear, rejecting spirituality, failure to find meaning in life beyond the physical, constant sense of frustration

If you'd like to talk or sing your way to balancing your chakras, you could string the chakra sounds together—*lam, vwam, ram, yam, ham, om,* and a *silent om* in that order. After you've gone through them as much as you like, you can do it one more time but backward to end up at the chakra connected to the earth so you feel grounded.

If you'd like to take some tests to find out which chakras need healing, there are a lot of chakra tests out there in books and online for you to discover which chakras are free and open and which need to be opened and unblocked for clarity and centeredness. Have fun learning a little more about your insides!

What about the outside? You already know that you radiate energy and that other people can sense it. You know how sometimes you meet someone, and before they even speak or look at you, you automatically like them or wish they'd go away? There are various possible reasons for this, but one of them might be that they're giving off positive or negative energy that you can sense on some level—even if you don't know what you're sensing.

If you sense it's negative, you don't have to run. Try being kind and see whether you can sense their energy changing. You might have a great chance to raise vibrations!

The energy you radiate is called your aura. Auras completely surround all living things.

Some people can see auras, and you might be happy to know you can train yourself to see them, too. Practice by softening your gaze on someone else, or on yourself in a mirror, and wait for the glow of light that appears around the body. If you keep at it, you might eventually see the colors of it flowing freely as well as where there is stuck or blocked energy. You wouldn't be wasting your time to practice this.

Auras are real and can be seen. Kirlian photographs show auras and prove that our energy fields change shape, size and colors to match what we're going through. The inner layers of the aura closest to the body connect with the physical body, and the outer layers connect with emotions, mental state and the spiritual self. The innermost layer is connected to the root, and from there, it goes in the same order as the chakras and the rainbow: red, orange, yellow, green, blue, indigo, violet.

Your aura affects your health in mind, body and spirit, and your health affects your aura. Your aura holds representations of everything you experience, including thoughts and feelings on conscious and unconscious levels. The energy patterns change as health and moods change.

Your aura changes size. If you have a lot of positive thoughts, feelings and experiences, it will extend further than if you're feeling negative. It might be about two or three feet on a bad day, but after a healing session, such as Reiki, it can extend thirty feet or more.

You can pass out positive energy with your healthy aura. It won't deplete if you share it—it's like a candle flame that way. It's not just your body—everyone and everything is energy.

Every*one* has a vibratory level, energetically speaking.

Every*thing* has a vibratory level, energetically speaking.

The vibratory level of objects is relatively low.

Your vibratory level is changing all the time.

Sit and think of the best feeling ever. What does it feel like? Take your time. Memorize it. Do you have it memorized already? Good job! Your vibe level is now higher! The happier, healthier, and more spiritually connected you become, the higher your vibes. You didn't have to memorize it to raise your vibes, but if you have memorized it, it'll be there for you anytime and anywhere.

There are lots of ways to do it, but you raise your vibrations every time you tune in to your higher self. And when you raise your vibrations, your fresh glow of happiness raises other people's levels of happiness. When their vibrations rise, they can go ahead and raise the vibrations of others. It goes on and on and on like a happy set of dominoes.

Energy is very powerful. You know it's true—you can see and feel it when someone's sadness or anger dampens the moods of everyone in the room. Good moods, thankfully, work in the opposite way.

Let's work with energy to make the world a better place! There are lots of ways to make the magic happen! Many people have been told since childhood to try harder, so you strive to do more, but what would really be helpful would be to go back to all that you already are and have been from the start. That's where your trueness is. That's where your whole self is. That's where your perfection is. Did you hear that? You're already perfect! Appreciate it.

Long-lasting happiness, peace and satisfaction come from your own heart and your own soul. Thinking that true happiness comes from outside of you just leads to blaming the wrong people for your problems, and that's not a long-lasting fix to anything. Freedom from unhappy emotions comes when you let go of desires and choose to be happy just because.

Here's a random list of ways I like to raise my vibrations: smiling, laughing, being in sunshine, walking on sand, making jokes, being positive, being with family and friends, being alone, vacationing, hiking, walking the dog, exercising, dancing a mix between the running man and the cancan, looking at stars, being in fresh air, listening to people being funny, looking at the moon, throwing away stress, dancing and singing to fun music, watching people breakdance, being my own best friend, keeping in touch with the divine, being with kids and elderly people, exploring nature, Donnie Wahlberg, Ellen, rapping, and writing rap songs. I threw those in because this is *my* list. You get to make your own happy vibes list!

Most retired people are very happy and lose a few wrinkles directly after retirement. That should help you realize that overworking is not the best way to live your life!

If you treat yourself like a good friend, you're nice to yourself and respect your thoughts and actions. If you're mean to yourself, you'll be miserable. Wouldn't you like to have a good friend with you everywhere you go? You can—you just have to be that friend to yourself.

Playing with your vibrations will teach you a lot about how energy works. You'll learn how you can heal physically, mentally and spiritually. You control how high your vibes go!

Since our physical bodies are generally at a low vibration, and spiritual energy is at an extremely high vibration, *most* of us can't see spiritual energy. Some can! Do you call those people crazy? I don't. I call them lucky. Soon, you could be one of them! Your superpower is that the law of vibration *will* work for you!

Playtime!
Watch Your Energy Vibes Spin Around

Play with a pendulum or tea bag over your chakras. Anywhere the pendulum swings slowly, your chakras are blocked or stuck. Hold on to it patiently and wait for each chakra to open and heal.

You'll be glad you did!

-Or-

Find a way to place the color of each chakra on the correct place of your body. Wear red shoes or pants, an orange belt, a yellow shirt, maybe a green pin, a blue scarf, indigo sunglasses, or a violet hat. You don't have to wear them all on the same day, but whatever floats your boat and balances your chakras is fine.

Where Are They Shooting?

Draw what you think your aura might look like at the moment and how it changes throughout the day for three days in a row.

-Or-

Spend time in front of a mirror to see a glow. Use a small amount of light—maybe a candle. Squint softly. Keep it up and notice if you begin to see colors after a while.

When you're done, draw a sketch of the colors that surround you.

You can then practice on other people. Once you have the knack, you'll be able to see auras around people on a regular basis.

Feel Those Vibes

Sit and feel your energy. Become aware of your energy vibrations as you go through your day. You don't have to do it constantly, but every time you think of it, feel it.

Once you're in the habit of noticing your vibes, change it up by making them move higher and faster in whatever way works for you on that particular day. Enjoy!

-Or-

Think about all of the things that make you happy. Write them down one thing at a time. Go ahead and include the little things that don't feel important. Just keep listing things one after another.

Wait! Notice how you feel in your mind, body, heart and spirit.

Okay, now go ahead and keep listing things that make you feel happy, grateful or lucky.

Keep going.

Keep going.

Keep going.

Great, huh?

Do you feel happier, more thankful, and luckier than you did before you started? If not, try it again. It really should work. Even if it doesn't last all day, it should last for a while.

Whenever the good feelings run out, try it again. You can also keep at it periodically throughout the day to keep you in happy vibe-land.

Here's the space for your own happy vibes list:

_____

_____

_____

_____

Imagination Leads to Meditation

Would you like to go to a land of make-believe? You can by going to your imagination!

Some spiritual leaders say not to use the term *imagination* because it's used as an excuse to claim that spiritual experiences aren't real. On the other hand, you can use your imagination as a way to achieve your spiritual experiences. Where do you think your imagination came from in the first place? Do you still use your imagination on a regular basis? What do you use it for? Think about it for a minute. What did you use it for when you were younger? Do you wish you still used your imagination as vividly? If so, do it! Why be bored?

You can create anything you want using your imagination. And you don't have to tell anyone how you're using your imagination to entertain yourself. It can be your secret. You wouldn't want anyone to think you're weird. Or, you could tell them what you're doing and let them think you're weird—and then remind them that it's more fun to be weird than it is to be boring! If you do tell people what you're doing, you might bridge the gaps between people. You'll also fit right in with some famous philosophers and scientists.

Think of fun things in your head to keep you entertained. What do you like? Sunshine? The ocean? Laughing with friends? I love when people tell me I'm funny, but I don't run around always trying to be funny to other people. Instead, I use my imagination to quietly say funny things to myself.

Whatever you do, find a way to make your days more enjoyable. You can use this technique to get through stressful situations, too. When I was young and had to get up in a room full of people, I was embarrassed at even the thought. I noticed some others were nervous too, and I noticed that some people weren't nervous at all. It occurred to me that they didn't know whether I was nervous or not, so I decided to pretend that I wasn't.

I totally pretended my way through that situation, and the pretend courage flooded in. I couldn't believe it worked! So, the next time I was nervous, I again pretended I was confident until I was actually confident and didn't have to pretend anymore. What a fabulous feeling! You can't tell me there's no such thing as *fake it till you make it*!

One day, I was feeling sad and realized I had nothing to actually be sad about. I decided that I'd feel happier if it were only sunny out. I wondered how that happiness would feel. I imagined the sun coming right out of the clouds, taking up the sky, shining on the trees and grass, and shining on me. I imagined how it would feel on my face, and I was instantly happy! I even felt my mouth curving up into a big cheesy grin.

Speaking of cheesy grins, grinning makes you feel happy. You can be in a glum mood, but if you fake a smile, you will literally feel the endorphins in your body bringing you joy. Try it. It's a scientifically proven fact that endorphins increase even with a fake smile, and that endorphins chemically make you feel happier.

Speaking of cheesy, I love Cheetos. One day, on my way home from work, I thought I should really have a big bag of Cheetos. I knew it wasn't the best choice I could make. I was about ten minutes away from the store, and I had to decide before I got to the intersection. So, I thought about it, in detail, and visualized everything about what it would be like to get those Cheetos.

In my imagination, I spent the money on them, opened them with two hands, dug into that glorious pile of yumminess, and ate three or four at a time. I imagined them in my mouth, on my tongue, the crunching between my teeth, the cheese dust coagulating on my tongue and in my cheeks, and the chewed goodness traveling down my throat.

For ten minutes, I imagined so much eating that I felt I must continue on to the feelings that would surely follow if it were really happening: stomachache, guilt, and being too full for dinner. Just as the shame was about to kick in, I turned right at the intersection and smiled a big, fat, non-cheesy grin that I had sidestepped the Cheetos choice. I felt so satisfied that I didn't even want them anymore. What a fun, guilt-free ride home that ended up being!

Another way you can use your imagination is by pretending you're filled with happiness in every cell of your body. You will feel that very happiness. Think about what causes bubbles of happiness within you and strive to let them flow through you anytime you choose. I imagine bubbles that form from carbonation in soda, but instead of the carbonation in soda, it's happiness in me.

Sometimes I pretend that I'm in heaven—not in a morbid way but in a beautiful way. I think heaven is amazing—without a worry in the world—and it has more than all the caring and comfort I can imagine.

You can use a different thought process if it works better for you. I like using the word *pretending* because I never thought I had a great imagination. I always thought meditation was difficult, but pretending always came easy. You can think of it as your imagination or as moving meditations. Since specific words and thoughts affect your flow of energy, pick what works for you.

I know a lot of people think they just don't have the ability to do this, but you do—I promise you. The obstacle is that it takes practice.

Scientifically speaking, your brain has a kind of factory of chemicals that can manufacture opiate-like substances, creating euphoria, bliss, and all that other good stuff. It can also manufacture chemicals that create stress and depression. Positive breeds positive, and negative breeds negative. Most of us have the power to choose, since they are our brains and all.

Philosophers such as Plato, Goethe and Avicenna discussed there actually being a world between the physical realm and the divine. In the *imaginal world,* imagination works as a mediator or a translator between humans and the spiritual realm.

Consider divine beings reaching down through the imaginal world to shape it and sustain it. Imagine humans reaching up through it for fantastic visuals and guidance. The theory is that imagination is a real place. If this is too much to believe, think of the imagination as being the bridge between you and your unconscious mind—it's all from the same source anyway.

Spirits in heaven are learning, discovering and experimenting. They filter information down to those of us who are willing and open to accepting the information from them! This is how many of the greatest writers of books and music ended up with successful works—some without even planning.

Think of your imagination as a friend who knows where to go. Stay open to going along. You can even allow yourself to be surprised.

I know of someone who has a habit of acting like everyone he meets is kind. Amazingly, people around him are more often kind than not. It makes sense when you think about it.

Jimmy Fallon uses the technique of acting like all his guests are funny. He's even said that it's his job to make his guests seem funny. You can see how he does it by watching his interviews. Most of his guests seem funny.

Here's to the power of your thoughts. If you were in an altered state of consciousness and someone told you there was a hot iron on your thigh, your brain, in its altered state, would believe it and react like there really was a hot iron on your thigh. Once your brain was done sending signals to your body, there'd be blisters on your leg!

Did you know that Albert Einstein used imaginary thought experiments to discover his theory of relativity? Other thought experiments include Schrodinger's cat, Laplace's demon, Newton's cannonball, the twin paradox, Avicenna's falling man, and the ship of Theseus. Thoughts are powerful! Use your imagination and watch miracles happen!

You could even imagine yourself temporarily going totally brainless. Don't you sometimes feel like your brain works too hard? Wouldn't it be fun to go brainless—even if just for a little bit? Can you imagine what it would be like to not have to think so much? Think about it for a while. Ha! Just joking.

The word *meditate* can be intimidating for lots of reasons. For one, it can seem like one more thing to *do*. Meditation means becoming unaware in order to become aware. So, let's just go brainless for a while. Doesn't that sound easier and more fun? Stop trying to think. Stop paying attention to your thoughts. Just let them be. This is not a good idea to do all the time. This is just for meditation time. Your brain thinks, and you need to let it keep doing its job, but it's healthy for it to have a break.

If you're set on the idea of clearing your mind from thoughts altogether when you're meditating, you might be putting too much pressure on yourself. Many people give up meditating because it seems impossible. The brain thinks; that's its job, so attempting to make it stop is difficult.

Think of your brain like a television with lots of channels. You have a problem channel, an anger channel, a joy channel, and other channels you happen to flip past. Do you tune in to your channels purposefully or by happenstance? It's your choice. When you meditate—at any time of the day and night—you can tune in to whatever channel of your mind you want. You can even turn it off! Even being unattached to what channel your thoughts are on activates cosmic energies and makes your spiritual energy flow.

You can practice when you're doing a mundane task like mowing the lawn. Let your brain rest, keep a focus on just mowing the lawn, or pick something specific that you want to focus on like love, happiness, funny jokes or whatever else you want.

When random thoughts come, just sit quietly and let them pass. Think of them like clouds. You don't try to grab and hold them, and you don't try to push them out of the way. If you notice them, you just let them pass.

You could also think of your thoughts like ripples in a pond that start in the center and then just flow away into stillness, unattached to where they started.

Have you ever heard people say they get their best ideas in the shower? Since showering is such a mundane activity, your intuition finally has a chance to surface. It's like a meditation. There are answers within you, and they are available to you as long as you spend time listening to your intuition. So, what I'm saying is … spend more time in the shower.

Or, let your brain think less and your spirit lead more. Here's to the power of you!

You know how everyone pretty much has their own view of how things happened in any situation? That's because everyone sees things through their skewed viewpoints. Maybe it's because our brain hemispheres are all unbalanced. Typically, when you're awake, one brain hemisphere is working harder than the other, and when you're asleep, one hemisphere is working harder than the other.

When you meditate, ta-da! Your brain hemispheres balance, and when your brain hemispheres are balanced, you see a more accurate view of reality. Just imagine if everybody meditated! Taking the time to meditate might take some of your hardships away without you even knowing it because those hardships would have become unnecessary. Wouldn't that be great?

For example, when I was brainlessly wandering through a bookstore, I thought my intuition was telling me to get a certain book. My rationalizing brain got in the way and said that I didn't need any more to read than I already had. Within weeks, there was an upsetting situation at work. I wondered what was making the person involved act the way she was and how I could handle the situation. I realized the answer would be in that book! I went back for it, and sure enough, it was the answer to a lot of my questions. Now I'm thanking this woman (not aloud, of course) for reopening the door to this book, but I wish I had listened to my intuition in the first place. Maybe I wouldn't have had to go through that. It would have been nice to avoid!

Some people think meditation is boring and takes too much time. It forces mind clutter to the surface so that you actually have to deal with your issues. How annoying! Do it anyway. It'll only feel icky for a while. Once you've gotten past that part, it'll become wonderful. After that, it'll become your natural way of experiencing yourself spiritually. Doesn't that sound glorious? You'll love it!

Reasons to Meditate

- It frees blocked energy, so you'll learn almost anything more easily and quickly.
- It connects you to your truth, which makes you truly happy, unlike the material things you hope will make you happy.
- It relaxes your body and mind so your spirit has time to emerge.
- It induces feelings of inner peace.
- It balances emotions.
- It alleviates anxiety and depression.
- It heightens your ability to cope with stress.
- It increases problem-solving skills.
- It helps you gain insights more readily.
- It increases awareness and a sense of clarity.
- It connects you with your breath.
- It promotes healing.
- It increases memory.
- It decreases the brain's aging process.
- It increases neural connections in your brain.
- It connects you to a higher aspect of self.
- It connects you with the divine.
- It makes you feel like you've been on vacation without leaving home!

Common Meditation Practices

- focusing on your breath
- focusing on an object, such as a candle flame
- being mindful of your thoughts and the environment without becoming attached
- guided meditation
- concentrated movement—slowing the movement of your hands, feet, arms and legs
- walking as slowly as possible to an endpoint
- journaling with no intention of content
- conscious eating—silently concentrate on where each ingredient came from, the smell of each ingredient, the taste of each bite, and chewing each bite a specific number of times
- repetitive prayers
- mantras
- asking for enlightened infusion and waiting for it

There's no required time for meditation, and you don't have to worry about controlling it. You're not even actually doing it. You're simply allowing it to happen. Wait for it. Be patient and forgive yourself if you don't see the benefits right away.

Meditation practice is very personal. Give yourself time to experiment and discover what resonates with you. It may be completely different from anything anyone else has tried, and it could be different for you each time you practice.

While meditating, you might not feel a whole lot—or you might feel quite a lot! You could feel warmth or coolness flowing through or over your skin. You might feel vibrations.

If you sit up without a backrest, the spiritual energy vibrations might have your upper body moving like your head is an inverted pendulum. Unfortunately, when people get to that point, they often wonder what's happening and quit meditating.

If you can deal with that new feeling, you'll be happy you did. You'll get deeper into your meditation, and it will open you up to the other side, which is more fantastical and heavenly. It is a practice. As long as you make an attempt, your body and mind will benefit from the experience. With repetition, you will succeed.

You can take meditation mini vacations for your brain. Choose an amount of time—maybe five or ten minutes each day—for a brain break meditation mini vacation. Choose one of these activities, sit back, close your eyes, relax your body and facial muscles, breathe, and focus.

Brain Break Meditation Mini Vacations

- The divine power has me on a silver cord like a yo-yo to keep me close.
- I'm original on purpose. It's better than if everyone were the same! I rock.
- Love in my heart is real. Fear in my head is what I don't know for sure, and it is an illusion.
- I replace worry with light.
- I'm here to learn to trust the higher power. If life were always easy, I wouldn't have to learn that trust.
- When I show patience, I trust the timing of the divine.
- When I have to wait, I'm happy for what's causing me to have to wait. It reminds me that I'm meant to be still sometimes.
- When I help someone, his or her prayer is being answered through me! I'm divine light for that person.
- I breathe into the light of my soul, and I realize that all I need is my divine nature.
- I let thoughts go and feel from my spirit where I feel radiant, loved, and whole because my spirit is perfect.
- My life is a dream, and my dreams are real.
- I live aloha with my open heart, loving mind and happy spirit.
- Being lonely even in a room full of people is a sign to find my true happiness in myself.
- When something I could perceive as bad happens, like if I walk through a spider web, instead of complaining, I'm just happy for a new experience.
- I see limitations as liberations; instead of resenting my pain, I use it as another reason to reach out to the divine.

- When I have an itch, I use it as an experiment to experience it. I decide on its color, brightness and density. I change the color, brightness and density with my thoughts until it changes and goes away.
- When I need to cry, I cry! Emotional toxins release—maybe even inviting others into my life to help me. When I'm done mourning, I can refocus and feel good again.
- I notice when I'm holding onto something that hurts, and then I do what I need to do to let it go so I can make room for something that feels good.
- I can go to the healing tower of the divine world anytime.
- I can be in touch with my body's healing powers anytime.
- When I want to change something about my life, I embrace it rather than trying to push it away so I can come to understand it and let it go.
- I remember the old saying about the richest person not having the most—but needing the least.
- Even if nothing good ever happens to me again, I feel blessed because I have my divinity. No one can stop my fate.
- When I feel empty, I fill up with all the love and peace the higher powers have been trying to pour into me.
- Life includes problems, but I get to choose how I handle them.
- I don't control the outside—the higher powers do. I control inside of me.
- I totally appreciate and spend time with my inner spiritual light.
- The beauty I see in others is a reflection of me.
- I will keep my feet, hands and tongue still. If my tongue is still, my eyes can be still. If my eyes are still, my mind can be still.
- The higher powers want me to be happy! I enjoy the path that is mine.
- When I'm meant to have answers, I'll have them.
- My thoughts make me happy because I'm my own best friend.
- When a dream dies, I dream another dream.
- When I give love, I get more love.
- I send love and light out into the universe so a light will go on in someone's soul. I know the love will be felt.

- If part of me is happy even when another part is sad, someone else who is sad will feel the energy of that love.
- I give up trying to please everyone. The higher powers could please everyone if they wanted to, but they don't because that's not the point of life—so I'm certainly not going to bother either!
- I focus on my real purpose and my passions. My passions aren't coincidence—they're my calling!
- When I'm jealous, I remember that if I could trade lives with anyone, I'd get their problems, too. I don't want the pains and troubles they hide.
- I smile for seemingly no reason because smiling tricks my body into feeling good—that's the way I was made on purpose.
- The divine power does not condemn me—so neither do I.
- I give my guilt to the divine light so it dissipates. That's the point of being forgiven.
- I focus on an object and count my breaths at the same time because it puts both hemispheres of my brain to work so they balance.
- If I stare at my left hand, my right brain stays busy so my thoughts settle down.
- When I want to emotionally disconnect, I think about a cord attaching me to the situation or person I want to disconnect from, and I imagine taking a huge pair of scissors and cutting the cord.
- I'm like wine—I get better with age. I'm getting better, smarter and happier.
- I let the shower clean my body on the outside and my spirit on the inside.
- I imagine washing my brain like it's in a washing machine. I scrub, scrub, and scrub to keep scum away.
- I refuse to take myself too seriously.
- I refuse to take things personally.
- I'm 100 percent myself. I experience what it's like not to conform.
- When I get home, I visualize dropping off all negative feelings from my day into a box, which stays outside of my home.
- I put all my yucky feelings into a rock (metaphorically) and throw it.

- When I hear terrible things on the news, I send healing, good vibes and love.
- I imagine being an ocean animal and watching the view deep in the water.
- I spend time talking to my divine faves, trusting that quiet moments with the higher powers transcend time and help me accomplish more.
- I live today and let tomorrow be for tomorrow.
- I imagine my guide singing a love song to me throughout the day.
- I treat everything like it has a spirit.
- Exercise is fun because it's my time to play and to be brainless.

You can write your own ideas for meditation here:

_____

_____

_____

_____

_____

If these things don't help you see miracles and magic, it's because you're still in your brain. Keep trying!

Playtime!
It's Always Playtime in My Imagination

Do you still use your imagination on a regular basis? What do you use it for? Think about it for a minute. If you answer the question here in writing, you can use your notes as a jump-start. Also, as you practice, you'll be able to see the changes you'll have made along the way.

_____

_____

_____

Now think and write about what you used your imagination for when you were younger.

_____

_____

_____

_____

_____

_____

(I thought you might need more lines for the second one!)

-Or-

Imagine the best friends possible walking or riding with you whenever you're feeling bored and playing with you no matter what you're doing—even when you're working hard.

-Or-

Imagine a friend or a guide giving you advice. Do this every time you need advice.

-Or-

Imagine yourself as the most fun person to talk to. Be your own best friend by using fun, uplifting inner dialogue.

-Or-

Change your inner dialogue to communicate with your spirit guides.

Big Time Brainless

Just let your thoughts go. You will keep thinking—that's your brain's job, so it's okay, but there are ways around those thoughts when you want to go brainless.

Think of your thoughts like grains of sand in a jar of water that you shake up and then set down so those thoughts settle down to the floor of the jar with no more movement.

There are other ways you can play around to be unattached to your thoughts.

Write ideas down here:

_____

_____

_____

_____

_____

Trippy Trippy

Imagine floating on a cloud like Aladdin's rug.

-Or-

Imagine spiritual light shining on you, particularly on your face, in your heart, and in your soul.

-Or-

Imagine a guide in front of you. Ask for advice and listen to your feelings for the answer.

-Or-

At random, pay detailed attention to your senses.

- Sight. Look at the views—or even a couch cushion or piece of grass.
- Touch. Feel what you're sitting or standing on.
- Smell. Breathe in even the faintest of smells.
- Hear. Listen to all the sounds close and far that are happening around you.
- Taste. What is on your tongue right now?
- Intuition. Is there anything there you recognize? If so, notice how it's coming to you so you can learn to listen to it.

Did your mind wander during this play period? Of course it did—you're in your human form! No problem! That'll happen. Just come back to it. After practice, notice how your mind wanders less and less.

Dump Dukkha Sleeping in Noni Trees

Because you're full of human energy—you're full of dukkha.

I'm full of dukkha.

We're all full of dukkha.

Let's dump it!

Although I love the word *dukkha*, the feeling is awful!

Dukkha is any negative feeling, big or small. It's any feeling of dissatisfaction, unfulfilled desire, discontent, restlessness or unhappiness, including adamant opinions you hold, obsessions, destructive habits, and anything else that causes you suffering, pain or bad feelings.

Dukkha is a very human thing, so you don't have to feel bad about yourself for having it, but we're going to work to get rid of it.

It's not easy to ignore because it's hard to shake. At the same time, letting it get the best of you does absolutely no good. Dukkha causes you to misperceive reality. You get so caught up in your own head that you have no idea what's really going on.

You might have an easier time identifying dukkha if you name it or can sing about it. Here's a song: Your name is Dukkha—you live on the bottom floor. I live upstairs from you—yes, I think I've met you before.

If you think it might help you, keep a dukkha list. If you do this, you're bound to see the same icky thoughts repeating on you.

The repetition on your dukkha list means it's a bad habit. Guess what you can do with bad habits? Change them!

After doing—or not doing—something seven times, it's a new habit. That's it! So, change up your habits and remember you only have to be successful seven times in a row before it's easy for you.

Here are the steps for change:

1. Realize you want to change.
2. Realize what causes you to do it in the first place.
3. Understand the benefits of changing it.
4. Explore your options.
5. Make new decisions.

6.   Make the change!
7.   Recognize whether you're changing successfully.

If at first you don't succeed, experiment with alternate behaviors.
Good job and congratulations—or keep trying!

Even when you make such positive changes, mindfulness and glimmers of enlightenment can be elusive.

Even though you can achieve them many, many times a day, you might not hold on to them for long because you get distracted and attached. Before you know it, you're experiencing dukkha all over again.

Congratulations—you're human! You have to keep working. Sorry, but that's what you've signed up for.

You have all the tools you need. With repetition and practice, you will get better and better at it. It will last longer and take up a bigger percentage of your time as you get better at it.

Other tools you can use to help you achieve glimmers of enlightenment and healing are found right here on our earth. Imagine what you would find on a tour of the Big Island of Hawaii!

On the Big Island of Hawaii, I met a noni tree. The leaves are large, and the fruit is yellow and bumpy. A tour guide told us yogis with sore calf muscles to wrap one leaf around each calf, tie them on with tube socks, and look forward to waking up in the morning with no calf pain. He was right about that!

When I awoke, I was amazed at the healing qualities of noni tree leaves.

I still had a problem, though. I was still sore everywhere else on my body!

That night, I had a fun dream that I was actually sleeping in a noni tree and being healed all over my body. I woke up feeling as vibrant as ever! How would you like to sleep in a noni tree? Imagine it healing everything that ails you. Talk about dumping your dukkha!

I was fascinated with the heavenly, holistic powers we can find right here, wherever we are, to heal ourselves, raise our vibrations, and get closer to the truth within ourselves and the universe.

There are other heavenly powers I've caught on to about the earth, and I can't even imagine how many more there are that I haven't realized yet. Think about holistic healing or natural healing as more of what you already know. It's like using ice for a swollen ankle or heat for stiff muscles. You know this stuff, but there's so much more to discover.

As you heal, you'll realize that you're like an onion. There are many layers to you and your issues. You heal one layer at a time.

One way to start is to make sure you are getting all the vitamins your body needs. The fruit of the noni tree, for example, is thought of as an elixir of life. It's full of vitamins B_1, B_2, B_3, B_5, B_6, B_{12}, C, folate, beta-carotene, calcium, potassium, magnesium, iron and phosphorous.

It does not taste good.

If you're not living out the dream in Hawaii where noni trees grow, or you just don't want to eat food that doesn't taste good, you might want to get a hold of the juice or supplement.

Benefits of Noni

- It gives you a regular sleep cycle.
- It gives you better immunity.
- It acts like a painkiller (including for arthritis).
- It helps mend bones and sprains.
- It restores the liver.
- It rejuvenates skin and hair by increasing collagen.
- It guards against type 2 diabetes.
- It gives you better blood flow and blood pressure.
- It raises your physical endurance.
- It boosts your energy.

And it's not just noni. Imagine a huge garden full of healing plants. If all the plants in the world that had healing qualities were in one garden, you would be flabbergasted by the size.

Back in the day, humans and animals knew how to use nature to heal all sorts of ailments. How do you think they got along before pharmaceuticals were invented? They got along just fine—that's how!

We can get back to it. When I think about it, I feel like we were really meant to be healthier and happier than we ever thought was possible. Have you ever heard of the healing oils used in the Bible? They were used to anoint people during prayer with the use of touch and with an intention of healing.

Since oils come from the essence of the plant, they're called essential oils. Essentially, oils are medicine provided by the same power that created the universe.

When pharmaceutical companies came along, they made medicine easier and faster. It seemed better. Unfortunately, even though doctors help us in so many ways, there are horrible side effects from many of the medicines we use.

It was a long time before people noticed the harmful side effects, and by then, a lot of our natural instincts had fallen by the wayside. Wouldn't it be better to get well without having to suffer side effects? Wouldn't it be better to get well without having to suffer from harsh chemicals? You can!

Modern medicines are still extremely valuable, and you shouldn't avoid doctors just because you're using oils. Also, doctors and scientists are finding more and more ways to heal more naturally, more from the earth. Lots of professionals are exploring the old ways of doing things and finding innovative new ways to make them work for us.

Either way, you're looking for balanced health, so learn what oils you could use and then use them in moderation. Overdoing things is often counterproductive.

Essential oils can be found in stores at a low cost, but the low-cost ones are diluted and manufactured with technology and chemicals. These are wonderful for the healing qualities of the aromas, but they are not medicinal.

If you're looking for deep healing, use therapeutic-grade oils because they are medicinal. They are uncompromised plant oils and not grown with pesticides, chemicals, additives or dilutions. They're also not exposed to extreme heat because when the oils get too hot, the healing qualities are essentially burned away, causing them to lose that therapeutic grade.

Therapeutic-grade oils cost more than diluted oils, but you get what you pay for. Plus, you can dilute them yourself with inexpensive carrier oils, such as pure vegetable oil from the grocery store or special complex oil, which you can buy from any therapeutic-grade essential oil company.

Therapeutic-grade oils are very strong. One drop of peppermint equals about twenty-seven cups of peppermint tea. Your therapeutic oils will go far because once you know how potent they are, you don't use much at any given time.

Depending on the oil and what you're using it for, you can diffuse, smell, ingest small amounts, or place them on your body.

The limbic system, the part of the brain at the forehead, stores memories and emotions. It is affected by the sense of smell, but not by other senses, so the oils tap deeply into the brain, mind, body and spirit. That leads to vibrational healing by influencing your life force energy, which tells the body where to heal. Smelling the oils leads to emotional releases and physical healing.

As soon as a person says the oil smells good, there's already a change happening. In fact, as soon as a person says it smells bad, there's already a positive change happening. In many cases, oil smells bad to a person because there's something within them that is off and needs healing. As soon as whatever it is heals, the oil will smell good to them. It's medicinal magic!

When you're using oils to heal yourself, be attentive to the ailment and to how you're feeling to know how often to reapply.

You might only need it once—or you might have to reapply throughout the day. Play and see what works for you. Put your intention into placing the oil and be present with it.

Placing oils on the bottoms of your feet heals you throughout your body because of the pathways that connect your feet to specific parts of your body.

Different oils can work differently for different people in the same way aspirin affects some people more than others. Keep this in mind with those who are more sensitive to the oils, especially babies, elderly people and animals. Usually they only need to smell it; application can cause problems on such sensitive beings.

Since all oils have different qualities, read the labels before you use them.

How Essential Oils Can Work for You

Lavender

Use this oil whenever you need something, but you're not quite sure what you need. It's the mother lode as far as the number of ailments it can help. It's deeply peaceful and relaxing, which benefits all parts of you. It affects your cardiovascular system, emotional balance, nervous system and skin.

It can be for ADD/ADHD, depression, anxiety, high blood pressure, pain, stretch marks, teeth grinding, wrinkles, acne, allergies, chapped lips, chicken pox, diaper rash, concentration, inflammation, insect repellent and more. That's quite a varied list!

Lemon

This oil is great for anxiety and is commonly used for autism. It's wonderful for cleaning the kitchen and bathroom. You can purify your water with it, and it helps you lose weight naturally as it purifies your body.

Citrus oils on your skin are photosensitive for about twelve hours. If you put them on your skin and hang out in the sun, you might see a color change. It will go away, but it's best to prevent it.

Lime

This is great for reducing fevers and sore throats since it works with your immune system. It also works with your digestive and respiratory systems. Since it's stimulating and refreshing, use it when you're tired, depressed, or want to improve your memory.

Use it around the house for removing gum, grease, or spots of oil.

Oregano

It can be used for cooking and for warts. Cool, huh? It's antibacterial, antifungal and delicious.

Peppermint

It's stimulating to the conscious mind and increases mental accuracy. It's great for curing hangovers, stomachaches, headaches, migraines, cold sores, asthma, motion sickness, tennis elbow, sore muscles and shock. It also clears sinuses.

Put a drop on your tongue and press it onto the roof of your mouth or rub it on your forehead and your feet. Another option is to put a drop in water—cold water or comfortingly hot.

Be very careful with peppermint around babies because it can take their breath away.

Ginger

Ginger is great for diarrhea, gas and indigestion.

Valerian

This is a depressant, which sounds terrible, but that doesn't mean it brings you depression. Instead, it helps you get a great night's sleep. It's great for helping you beat insomnia.

Frankincense

The soul gravitates to frankincense and releases negativity. It's a balancing energy, and it's an antidepressant. Since it's a spiritual oil, using it on the feet before bed can bring meaningful dreams.

It has cured fevers, ringworm, mysterious rashes, and in some cases, cancer—though through a very elaborate process.

Myrrh

It promotes spiritual awareness and is uplifting. It affects the skin and the hormonal, immune and nervous systems.

There are a lot more essential oils that you can blend to make even more cures. Different oils and blends work differently for different people. You might want to experiment to see what works for you.

To make a sickness defeater, you could use a mix of clove, lemon, cinnamon bark, eucalyptus radiata, and rosemary cineol. You can ingest it or put it on the bottoms of your feet. Essential oil companies have similar blends sold under different names.

Other good mixes are available for joyful giggle fests, deodorant, pain relief during surgery, sciatica, bone pain, arthritis, sprains, muscle spasms, bruises, frostbite, chiropractic alignment, getting rid of mosquitos, mosquito bites, and much, much more.

Here's to oiling your vibrations!

Playtime!
Dump Your Dukkha

Doling out the dukkha… What's your dukkha? List it all. Make it a game to not think about the things on your list for a whole day, a week, or as long as you can go.

At the end of each day, give yourself three stars if you succeeded morning, noon and night. Give yourself two stars if you succeeded morning and afternoon but slipped back into it at night. Give yourself encouragement to try again if you don't have three stars! It's a practice. You might not have many stars in the beginning of the game, but you'll find your stars piling up if you keep at it.

-Or-

Next time you're in an uncomfortable situation, try acknowledging the situation while refusing to acknowledge the suffering part.

-Or-

Let go of your expectations and notice everything becoming a new experience.

Sleep in a Noni Tree

Take an Epsom salt bath with various essential oils. Let it draw out your toxins and renew you with health and happiness.

Fruity Fun

Find out what nutrients are in the fruits you eat today. Extend it by finding out what nutrients are in all of the food you eat in one day.

Groovy Garden

Get an aloe plant. Find out how to help it grow and how to use it to heal some of your pains. See how well it works for you!

-Or-

Draw a picture of heaven's gardens, animals, landscapes and divine beings. As an abstract bonus, draw the love. I bet you can't quite capture it!

You're a Lotus on an Eightfold Path

Lotus flowers grow out of mud!

You might look out yonder and see nothing but mud in front of you, and right seemingly out of nowhere a beautiful flower is reaching its petals out to remind you that beautiful things grow out of muddy situations.

The lotus flower is used as a symbol in yoga to show that beautiful circumstances can grow out of the pain and agony in our lives.

The yoga lotus position is sitting with your legs folded under you—you are the flower that grows within and rises out of your suffering. You don't have to have your legs folded under you. As you sit quietly, imagine yourself as a lotus flower. You grow beautifully out of all the muddy situations in your life. The muddier it is, the more beautifully your soul grows!

The word *yoga* means *yoke*, which means to connect and unite. Yoga is described as a science that frees the mind. Yoga has been around for a very long time, but it wasn't always very popular in many parts of the world. In the 1960s, the Beatles and other musicians and movie stars made it more widely accepted after going to India to explore transcendental meditation. They found it beneficial and brought yoga to America.

A lot of people think of yoga as a physical exercise, but it is so much more than that. Yoga is a way to balance the three parts of you: mind, body and spirit. In yoga practice, you do this by mastering the mind and the body so that spiritual energies can flow more freely. One of the main reasons to practice yoga is to connect with your true self, without judgment, and to connect with the divinity within yourself.

During our day-to-day routines, our minds and bodies take over, and our spiritual selves sit quietly waiting to be there for us if we choose. If the spirit is not called upon enough to balance you, it leads to energy blocks that can show up as mental fatigue, emotional strains and physical pain. Part of yoga's purpose is to train your brain to think healthy thoughts and relax so your spirit has more time to take over.

During a yoga practice, you master your body through simply holding or moving through poses, or *asanas*, while you breathe deeply and slowly. You can challenge your body in your poses, but you don't need to strain your body. If you feel a pain that could lead to injury, don't do it. Your yoga is meant for you. No matter what the teacher says, listen to your body! And I say this as a yoga teacher.

The control of the breath helps master your mind, which is done best by clearing the mind of thought. It sounds tough because it is, but don't worry about that. It's called practice for a reason. It takes time and is never perfected for most people. Every little bit of practice helps a lot—so keep it up.

One trick is to set an intention or think about one specific thing that makes you feel good. For example, you might focus on a feeling of happiness, peace, love, positive vibes, fresh air, spreading magic, or healthy energy. You name it. Choose your one thing, breathe it in deeply, imagining it flowing right through every part of you, and exhale slowly, imagining it flowing through every part of you. Throughout your asana practice, keep your mind on this breathing practice as much as possible.

When you notice your mind wandering, let it go and come back to your intentional breath. There is no need to berate yourself when your mind wanders. A thinking brain is a normal and healthy thing, and getting down on yourself for it is counterproductive toward finding peace and balance of mind, body and spirit.

In mastering your mind and body, your spirit will most definitely emerge. It is there—and it is emerging—even if you don't realize it. You might not feel a thing. You might feel like it isn't working for you or think you're not good at it, but it is working, and you're a gem!

If you do feel it, it might take any or all of the following forms:

- the body feeling lighter
- the mind feeling clearer
- a warm, subtle tingling
- a sudden sense of security in who you are
- peace
- joy
- balance

Whatever you feel, it's the feeling that's meant just for you. Yoga is not meant to conform you. Yoga is not a religion. Yoga accepts all religious beliefs. Some religious beliefs have inspired various parts of the yoga practice, and that is why you may hear some religious connotations during a yoga class. However, it is never meant to force any type of belief on anyone.

There are many types of yoga classes. Some are simply called yoga and provide poses and breathing practice. You can seek out specialized classes, however, which include:

- *Hatha.* General asanas, breathing and meditation
- *Vinyasa.* A flow of poses, moving with the breath
- *Restorative.* Asanas that are held for longer periods (about ten minutes)
- *Hot.* Poses in a heated room to encourage sweating
- *Yin.* Quiet and intense
- *Children's.* Poses with playful movement and playful words
- *Kundalini.* Meditative breathing techniques that leave you feeling high
- *Nidra.* Being still (also called sleep yoga)
- *Power.* High-energy muscle work
- *Disco.* Asanas with dance breaks
- *Death Metal.* Asanas with periodic yelling
- *Naked.* Naked yogis doing yoga

Yes, you read that right. You can probably find naked yoga classes closer to home than you realize.

It's okay for people to make up their own yoga. There's room for all kinds of yogis in the world. Don't listen to people who say, "That's not real yoga." They're wrong, and that's really just their closed-minded opinion. Change is good, and we should be open to accepting and celebrating anyone and everyone who is setting out to balance the mind, body and spirit in any way they see fit.

At the end of your yoga class, you'll likely hear the word *namaste*. What does it mean?

- The light in me honors the light in you.
- The divinity within me salutes the divinity within you.

- I honor the place in you that is of love, light, truth and peace.
- I honor the place in you where the entire universe dwells.
- When you are in that place in you, and I am in that place in me, we are one.

Yoga is an awesome way to do yourself some good. Do it for your body. Do it for your mind. Do it for your spirit. Balancing these three will help center you, help you reach your soul, and help you reach your truth.

The philosophy behind the yoga practice comes from a guidebook called the *Yoga Sutra*. It was written by Patanjali and contains an eightfold path referred to as the eight limbs of yoga.

Basically, the eight limbs of yoga are eight steps that act as guidelines for how to live a meaningful and purposeful life. Each step prepares you for the next step. The steps are kind of like a prescription for health and acknowledging your spiritual side. They're meant to help you turn your attention inward by promoting morals, ethics and self-discipline.

The first step, or limb, of the eightfold path is called *Yama*, which is the word for ethical standards:

- ahimsa: nonviolence
- satya: truthfulness
- asteya: nonstealing
- brahmacharya: self-restraint
- aparigraha: non-hoarding

The second limb is called *Niyama*, and it has to do with self-discipline and spiritual observances:

- saucha: keeping your mind and body clean and pure
- samtosa: appreciating what you have
- tapas: keeping your soul pure
- svadhyaya: enjoying your own divinity
- isvara pranidhana: surrendering to a higher power so you no longer suffer from your own mental condition

The third limb of yoga is called *asana*, which means pose. Asanas are the physical yoga poses. A lot of people think there's such a thing as being good at yoga, which unfortunately leads people to believe there is such a thing as being bad at yoga. There is no such thing!

Yoga poses are not about being able to touch your toes. They are actually about being with the self in a way that helps you get in touch with your soul. There are a ton of physical benefits to stretching, but yoga is not meant to be a competitive sport.

Pranayama is the fourth limb. Pranayama is breath control, and the energy inside the breath is used for clarity and connecting mind, body and spirit. You can use your breath throughout the day, on and off the yoga mat, to help you keep control over your body, mind and emotional reactions.

When practicing the fifth limb, or *Pratyahara*, we detach or withdraw our senses from things that are happening outside of us. We remain aware of our senses, but we direct our attention inward.

Would it irritate you if someone in your yoga class came in late while you were in the zone? Let irritations around you become instruments to help you practice balance within your own self and your own mind and soul. Then you can let it all go.

Do you get upset when you watch the news? Detach your senses and direct your attention inward.

The sixth limb of yoga is called *Dharana*, and it deals with the distractions of the mind itself. Choosing one thing to focus on can help you let go of distracting thoughts. Keep your focus, and when you feel your thoughts drifting away, just bring it back to this one focus.

The seventh limb is *Dhyana*, which is meditation or uninterrupted flow of concentration. It's being aware without focusing. This is a quiet mind.

The eighth and final stage of the eightfold path is *Samadhi*, which is a state of consciousness and total liberation. Patanjali described it as a state of ecstasy. A yogi in the eighth stage realizes the true interconnectedness that exists between all living things, the universe, and the divine, and therefore realizes a true sense of peace, wholeness and enlightenment.

You're not expected to master all of this, especially not right away. Start from where you are. Do you suffer from anxiety? Try some alternate nostril breathing for three to five minutes.

Alternate Nostril Breathing

Using your thumb and finger, close one nostril, inhale, switch nostrils, exhale, inhale, switch nostrils, exhale, and continue repetitively. Alternatively, close one nostril, inhale and exhale, and continue by alternating nostrils from there.

If you want to take it further, take three or more deep, slow breaths in each of the following poses:

- *Downward-facing dog.* With your hands and the balls of your feet on the floor, spread your fingers and distribute your weight around the outside of your palms (so it's not just on your wrists). Lift your hips up and back, and direct the armpits gently toward the floor.
- *Cat/cow.* From tabletop (on your hands and knees), allow your body to move with the pace of your breath, inhaling your head up while drawing your belly toward the floor (cow), and then exhaling your head down while pulling your back up toward the sky (cat).
- *Child's pose.* Bend your knees, rest your hips on your feet, and rest your forehead on the floor.

Repeat as needed.

If you have high blood pressure, you can do alternate nostril breathing as described above. If you want to take it further, take three or more deep, slow breaths in each of the following poses:

- Stand and fold forward with your hands reaching toward the floor or resting on something (such as your opposite elbows or the floor).
- Triangle pose with your feet spread with one leg in front of the other, while your nose reaches gently toward your front knee. (Spend the same amount of time with each leg).
- Child's pose (as described above).
- Bridge, which has your feet, upper back, head and hands on the floor while your hips reach up high.

To help mend a broken heart, try any pose that has your chest—where your heart is—reaching toward the sky. Take three or more deep, slow breaths in standing arm stretches, or try an upright pigeon pose on each side, where one leg is folded underneath you while your torso and head are raised up high. You could also do bridge with a block underneath your hips, so you can rest on it.

Do you want to prevent wrinkles? Take three or more deep, slow breaths in any pose that has your head upside down, like downward dog.

Downward dog helps with many other ailments, including:

- sinus issues
- bronchial congestion
- common colds
- headaches
- back pain
- poor circulation
- respiration problems
- anxiety and depression

Try some yoga poses each day, even if you don't know what poses go with your ailments. They can help keep you healthy when you're feeling good. You'll most likely benefit from doing any pose that doesn't cause injury.

Do you wish you made more time for yoga? Right now, what parts of your life seem to take over most of your day? What do you wish you had more time for? A lot of people say work or taking care of others takes up most of the day, and spending quiet time alone is not something a lot of people find time for.

Where's the balance? Do you wish you had more time? It isn't actually as much an issue of time as it is an issue of balancing work, home and play. You owe it to yourself, and you deserve to be taken care of. You have to take care of you. Curing yourself is all about finding balance between your mind, body and spirit. To have balance within yourself, it helps to have balance in your life.

If you have a balanced life, you'll feel okay about leaving work at work, going home to be with your kids while they grow up, and relaxing in whatever form works for you. For one, you don't have to check work emails when you're not at work. You don't even have to check your phone every time it dings.

Put you first by finding balance, and find balance by putting you first. You might even muster up enough courage to make a big life change like switching careers to something that works better for your life balance or moving across the globe to feel happier within your soul.

This is big-scale stuff, so what about the smaller-scale stuff, like when you're just feeling crabby for seemingly no reason? What do you do when you're crabby? It's tough enough to find balance when you're in a good mood, and it's even tougher when crabbiness creeps in. Next time you're crabby, think about what you're grateful for. It may sound cheesy, but it works. If you're thinking about things you're grateful for, you're too busy to concentrate on negative thoughts. It should brighten your mood and raise your vibrations. We're all different, but you can't really think two thoughts at once. As long as you're thinking about what you're grateful for, you'll be happy!

Find whatever works for your balance of mind, body and spirit.

Simply paying attention to your breath will help you achieve balance.

Prana is the life force energy of breath, and *yama* means self-control. *Pranayama* is when you control the breath, expand the breath, and bring conscious awareness to the breath.

Wherever you are and whatever you're doing, you can practice pranayama. When you're sitting with friends or are out and about, randomly make sure you're taking full breaths with each inhale. Let your breath all the way out on your exhales.

Notice where in your body you can feel your breath. Is it in your throat? Neck? Chest? Stomach? Your breath is likely to be shallower than you've realized, and when you're in a stressful situation, it becomes even shallower.

Viruses and bacteria grow more easily when we breathe shallowly because the oxygen isn't there to help keep them from invading our systems. You know how they say we only use a certain small percentage of our brain? We also only use about 20 percent of our lung capacity.

Breathing rate affects your mood, and your mood affects your breathing rate. When you're multitasking or feeling anxious, it's important to check in with your breath. If you're involved in a stressful conversation, your breath will quicken. If you calm your breath by making it slow and deep, your body and mind will also feel calmer.

When someone's irritating you, your blood pressure might rise. Instead of letting that happen, check in with your breath and center yourself in your peace and let your own love spread through you. If you have it in you, let your love energy silently spread to the person who is irritating you. You might be amazed to see how your energy affects others.

All you need to do is pay attention to it and practice deeper, more mindful breaths.

When we practice slow, mindful, full-capacity breathing, we help a more adequate supply of oxygen get to all of the organs and cells of the body. This leads to all sorts of good things, including a stronger immune system and a calmer, more peaceful, and more positively energized state of mind.

Breathing exercises improve:

- blood oxygen levels, carbon dioxide removal, and blood and nutrient flow to organs
- respiration, circulation and digestion
- immune system and pain management
- physical fitness levels, strength and posture
- vitality, including slowing the aging process of the skin
- mind, body and spirit connection
- stress and anxiety levels
- sleep quality and rejuvenation
- energy levels, alertness, awareness, attention, consciousness and mental focus
- presence of mind and mood
- inner peace and emotional calmness
- relaxation and meditative or trancelike states
- expansion
- connection to the calm, quiet place within, leading to an increased level of overall well-being
- connection with your inner, true self

If you sit, relax, and count your breaths, you can figure out how close you are to the average amount of breaths taken per minute. The average resting respiratory rate for adults is between twelve and twenty breaths per minute.

The average for middle-aged children is between sixteen and twenty-five, and the average for preschool children is between twenty and thirty.

During breathing exercises:

- Keep your spine as straight and long as possible.
- Close your eyes softly.
- Inhale and exhale through the nose. Nose hairs filter, purify, humidify, warm, and moisturize the air.
- Increase your practice gradually. Just like with any exercise, you don't want to do too much at one time.

Play with Your Breath

- Practice taking only six breaths per minute for a few minutes per day.
- Take as few breaths as you can during one minute without holding your inhale or exhale.
- Lie on your back with your knees up, place one hand on your stomach, and notice if the breath feels shallow or uneven. Make the breath smooth and relaxed and observe what your hand feels.
- Inhale to the count of four, including pauses where stated. Inhale … (count slowly to yourself while you're inhaling) one, two, three, four, pause … one, two, three, four, exhale … one, two, three, four, pause … one, two, three, four, repeat.
- Close your mouth and contract the muscle in the back of the throat during the exhale (like you're trying to fog up a mirror or pretending you're Darth Vader). Once you're able to make the sound with your exhale, try it with your inhale. Allow your focus to be on the sound.
- Inhale while raising your arms overhead and opening your palms and fingers, exhale with your arms still overhead, inhale again, then exhale forcefully while bending your arms and thrusting them down while making fists. Repeat this ten times without the extra inhales and exhales overhead. Instead, just inhale fully with your arms overhead while holding the breath for a count of five,

and then exhale forcefully while bending your arms and thrusting them down while making fists.

Be careful with these, or skip them altogether, if you have any issues that would make them counterproductive. As with any other practice, use them in moderation and as a way to find balance.

It's not necessary to always be conscious of your breath. All it takes is periodically practicing breathing exercises throughout the day. No matter how simple and short-lived they are, do yourself that huge, easy, all-important favor!

Playtime!
Loony Lotus

Be a lotus. Sit. Stay. Smile. Do this for five minutes. Tomorrow—repeat.

Chillin' on the Island of Your Yoga Mat

Let me lead you through a short yoga practice:

- Be still and breathe.
- Set your intention and make yourself a promise to stick to it throughout the entire practice. Make sure your intention is simple; it could be to focus on your breath, for example.
- Downward facing dog with your hands and the balls of your feet on the floor, fingers spread with the weight evenly distributed around the outside of the palms so it's not just on your wrists, lift the hips up and back while you direct your armpits gently toward the floor. Hold for at least one full in-and-out breath cycle.
- During an exhale, walk your feet up to your hands for a forward fold. Hold this for at least one full in-and-out breath cycle.
- During an inhale, stand up and reach up to the sky for an extended mountain pose.
- During an exhale, fold back down to a forward fold.
- Inhale as you hold your pose.
- During another exhale, move your feet back to downward dog. Feel your body as you direct your hips up and back and your armpits gently and slightly closer to the floor.
- Inhale deeply in downward dog.
- During an exhale, move to plank with your body straight with your ankles, hips, shoulders, and head all in line with your spine. If you choose, place your knees on the floor instead.
- Inhale as you hold plank.
- On another exhale, move very slowly to the floor for chaturanga.
- Breathe in as you push your palms into the floor, raising your shoulders partway or all the way up while leaving your hips and chest low.
- During an exhale, move to downward dog.
- Inhale in downward dog.
- During another exhale, move to forward fold.

- Inhale to extended mountain.
- Exhale one foot up to the side of your other leg (but not pushing into the side of your knee) for a tree pose.
- Keeping your arms up or putting your palms together at your heart center, inhale deeply and exhale slowly as you hold your pose for as long as you like.
- Repeat for your tree pose on the other side of your body.
- Inhale your arms up for extended mountain as both feet stand on the floor.
- Exhale your arms down.

That's a sun salutation with a balancing pose. Repeat as you like, noticing how you feel both before and after your practice so you can feel yourself healing through your moves.

Crazy Eights

Think about how you feel about each of the following:

- violence
- stealing
- dishonesty versus honesty
- keeping material things that you don't need or really want
- appreciating what you have
- holding yourself back from being mean
- keeping your mind, body and soul clean and pure
- enjoying your own divinity
- physical yoga poses to get in touch with your soul
- using the energy in your breath to control your body, mind and emotional reactions to connect your mind, body and spirit
- being unattached to your senses from things that are happening outside of you
- choosing one thing to focus on to help you let go of distracting thoughts
- meditation with a quiet mind
- surrendering to a higher power so you no longer suffer from your own thoughts
- total liberation, appreciating the true interconnectedness that exists between all living things, the universe, and the divine, and realizing a true sense of peace, wholeness and enlightenment

Cure Me Like Crazy

When you're being a lil' yogi chillin' on your yoga mat, notice how you feel before and afterward. That way, if say you have a headache, you might notice that downward dog helps your headaches go away. Then, next time you have a headache, you'll know to make time for a downward dog.

Big Top Balancing

Practice physical balancing acts (making sure to do both legs!):

- Lift one leg and move it in circles.
- Lift one leg and move your arms in circles.
- Lift one leg and move your ankle in circles.
- Stand on your tiptoes.

-Or-

Write down a list of the things that are important to you to spend time on each day. Then, make it a point to spend at least some time on one or all of them every day. You owe it to yourself!

_____

_____

_____

_____

_____

Batty Breaths

Notice how you feel in your body, mind, heart and spirit. Breathe in deeply and out slowly. Make sure your exhale comes out all the way before your next inhale. Repeat multiple times. Then notice how much better you feel.

Use this as your go-to as often as possible. This is a great one for anytime, anywhere.

-Or-

Count your breath cycles. One deep inhale followed by one slow exhale counts as one cycle. Keep counting. See how high you get before you forget and your mind wanders off of your breath. You'll notice your number getting higher and higher.

Write your numbers here:

Date   Time   Number of breaths

_____/_____/_____

_____/_____/_____

_____/_____/_____

_____/_____/_____

_____/_____/_____

_____/_____/_____

_____/_____/_____

_____/_____/_____

Great work!

Hear *This!*

Sing your song proudly because sound vibrations heal. And you don't have to be a musician or have a good voice for your sounds to raise your vibrations. The vibrations in your body move to match the vibrations of what you're listening to. When you listen to pleasant sounds, your body becomes more balanced and healthier.

When you listen to disturbing sounds, like city traffic or anger in someone's voice, your inner vibrations become more disturbed. Do you spend your days listening to people who complain a lot or bicker with each other? Negative sounds like those negatively affect your energy centers, and harmonic sounds positively affect your chakras.

You can experiment with training your brain to think in rhythmic affirmations. *Mantras* are sounds that help your mind feel freedom. The syllable *man* means mind, and *tra* means freedom. The sounds of the words in a mantra bring peace of mind. The meanings of the words elevate the mind. Free your mind and the rest will follow! Do you recognize *that* song? Think of mantras as songs or jingles that you can put on repeat in your head as you happily sing your way through your day.

During the normal parts of your day, one hemisphere of the brain works harder than the other. Meditating aloud with mantras, which is called chanting, synchronizes the hemispheres, slows the breath and relaxes the mind.

Chanting allows time for inspiration and for intuition, and it gives you a sense of connection with spirits in heaven and other people who are searching for connection with the divine.

Always use positive, or affirmative, words for mantras. There are parts of our brains that literally do not register negatives such as the word *not*. Ask for what you want instead of what you don't want. Otherwise, you might think you're asking to not get a headache, but since parts of the brain don't register the word *not*, you're actually sending your brain the message to get a headache. Ouch!

Chanting can be done in any language. Have you ever heard of *kirtan* music? Many of the songs that are chanted in kirtan music are in the language of Sanskrit. The word *kirtan* means "mantras being chanted." In Sanskrit, the meaning of the words is more important than the pronunciation, so don't worry if you don't know how the words are pronounced. Sanskrit is meant to have a very fluid sound. In fact, in its original language, it was sung.

Possible Chanting Themes

- Let go.
- I am peace.
- I am love.
- I am light.
- I speak my truth.
- I speak from my heart.
- I am part of the divine.
- I am my own best guru.
- I rock just as I am.
- I shine for all to heal from.
- I am a ray of sunshine to help others be happy.
- I radiate positive vibes onto those around me.

Sanskrit Meanings

Shanti: Peace.

Aum or *om:* This can be chanted with each letter being like its own syllable, but the Sanskrit pronunciation is *om*. Neither is wrong. The sound is a call to the divine and connects you to the vibrations of the universe, waves on a shore, leaves rustling, the inside of a seashell, beating hearts, and everything else in nature. The pieces of the om symbol represent the transcendental self, the dreaming state, the state beyond dreams, the waking state, and the veil of material illusion.

Namaste: The divine in me honors the divine in you.

Ganapati: The aspect of the divine that removes obstacles.

Namaste Ganapati: I honor the remover of obstacles.

Hare Krishna: This chant gives peace, happiness, wealth and concentration. Krishna is a name for the highest divine power.

Ananda: Extreme happiness.
Ki Jay: I have victory within me.
Maha Mata: Great Mother.
Durga: The invincible.
Lokah: The world.
Aja Ke: That I have in me.
Akhanda: Indestructible.
Samastah: May all beings be free from suffering.
Shakti: The Divine Mother.
Guru: A spiritual leader. (You are your own best guru.)
Deva: A divine being.

You can use the terms to piece together whatever mantra suits you best. Can you piece together the meaning of this mantra?

Om Guru Om Guru—Deva Deva
Om Guru Om Guru—Deva Deva
Aja Ke Ananda Ki Jay, Aja Ke Ananda Ki Jay

There are also *bija* mantras. Sounding out the bija mantras, or chanting, is a wonderful way to have a healing meditation. The word *bija* means *seed.* Chanting the bija mantras honors where you came from, which is your true home of heaven. Bija mantras are special sounds that resonate with each of the chakras.

Mudras are hand positions that go along with each mantra to help strengthen your meditation. Here are the sounds, the hand positions, and what you should visualize to heal your chakras:

- *Lam.* Palms up, connecting tips of pinkie fingers to thumbs (healthy root).
- *Vwam or Vam.* Palms up, connecting tips of ring fingers to thumbs (healthy sacral).
- *Ram.* Palms up, connecting tips of middle fingers to thumbs (healthy solar plexus).
- *Yam.* Palms up, connecting tips of pointer fingers to thumbs (healthy heart).

- *Ham.* Fingers stretched out next to each other, thumbs in palms (healthy throat).
- *Om.* Open palms, fingers and thumbs (healthy third eye).
- *Om (repeated, whispered, or silent).* Open palms, fingers and thumbs (healthy crown).

Have you ever heard whale sounds used for meditation? Whale sounds are similar to bija mantras because the vibrations can make you feel peaceful to your core just like the whirring of tree leaves, ocean waves slapping the shore, and other sounds in nature.

If you try your best to surround yourself with vibrational sounds that match the heart of the universe, your heart and soul will rise. Singing bowls make beautiful sounds like musical bells, and they are used to clear energy blockages with vibrations that soak into your being. These vibrations balance your chakras and match with and align your mind, body and spiritual energies for healing.

Considering that your chakras affect the health of your entire being, surrounding yourself with the harmonic sounds of singing bowls, especially in place of negative sounds, will make you feel better all around. You could play the music at work or at home. If you choose to do this, it will be like meditating. The left and right hemispheres of the brain will become synchronized just like after any other type of meditation.

Singing bowls raise your vibrations in such a simple way. All you have to do is hit the bowl and let the vibrations soak into you. If you buy a singing bowl or a cymbal for your own use, simply tap the side—using no special talent whatsoever—or learn how to tap and apply moving pressure for a more expansive sound. You could also sit in the same room while someone else hits the bowl! If you get a group of people who all know how to make rhythms together, it becomes even more powerful.

You might notice singing bowls being used in music in your yoga or meditation practice, music therapy, or sound healing workshops. The bowls are played with a mallet.

You could attend a singing bowl session, which might be called sound healing, a singing bowl bath, or a sound bath, where singing bowls are played harmonically. All you do is listen and let the vibrations soak into you. You will feel deeply centered and at peace with yourself and the world around you.

Whatever kind of music you like, listen to it! Your vibes will begin to match the vibes of the music. If the vibes of the music make you happy, you'll be filled with happy vibes.

Much of the mainstream music in our world is awesome, but depending on your preferences, it might leave you less than inspired to live with your heart and soul, especially if you're sensitive to the energy others are projecting. You might be more sensitive to negative connotations than you realize. If you love music but find that the lyrics bring you down and you're looking to be uplifted, there are a lot of fun alternatives.

You can listen to yoga music with lyrics. There are many heartwarming, uplifting, and fun songs—even the Grammy Awards get in on it. You can find radio stations filled with fun, wholesome songs about grace, forgiveness, letting go, and hope. If you want to tune in to Christian radio stations, you don't have to be afraid of what the word *Christian* means. Everyone has their own meaning, and some have negative connotations for no real reason. There's a variety of rock, rap, and more, and many of the songs are upbeat. You can jam out, learn the words, sing along, and feel uplifted at the same time.

For other sound healing, you can laugh like it's funny!

When I was a kid, I asked my grandma, "What's your favorite sound?" She said laughter. I loved that answer. Have you heard that laughter is medicine?

There were studies for which groups of patients were prescribed certain amounts of laughter each day. Wouldn't you know? There were radical differences in their levels of healing.

Once upon a time, a kid was playing basketball and broke his hand. He cried. Then he decided to stop crying and start laughing! That's weird, right? Well, maybe not. When he was asked about it later, he said he noticed his hand didn't hurt as much when he was laughing!

I've always known that smiling and laughing made me feel better. You know it, too. It seems so obvious, yet how often do you really laugh? How often do you hear other people laughing? Not enough!

The science of facial expressions shows that smiling and laughing come from our unconscious minds, which means that expressing feelings actually comes more naturally than hiding them. Laughter and facial expressions are natural. Blind children who have never seen other people's facial expressions have the same range of facial expressions as sighted people.

The ability to laugh is a gift! There are just too many benefits of laughing to ignore:

- Laughter is a natural painkiller.
- Laughter relaxes muscles.
- Laughter causes changes in the brain.
- Laughter boosts moods by releasing endorphins in your brain.
- Laughter beats away stress.
- Laughter boosts your immune system.
- Laughter involves breathing changes that have the same benefit as breathing exercises.
- Laughter stimulates lung health by increasing oxygen intake.
- Laughter balances blood pressure.
- Laughter is an aerobic exercise.
- Laughter improves heart function.
- Laughter gives similar results to a runner's high.
- Laughter boosts energy levels.
- Laughter creates a positive mental state for dealing with negative situations and negative people.
- Laughter improves digestion.
- Laughter improves memory.
- Laughter improves sleep.
- Laughter makes you feel more vibrant.
- Laughter gives you optimism and hope.
- Laughter is a type of meditation because it forces you to live in the moment.
- Laughter connects you with others and improves relationships.
- Laughter creates a happy feeling that stays with you.
- Laughter helps you attract happier friends.
- Laughter helps you respond better to problems because it changes the way your brain thinks of problems.

When I taught middle school writing and health, I gave smiling and laughter journals to my students and asked them to write specific details about how smiling and laughing throughout the day made them feel and how it affected others. It was the most fun writing assignment to read! And it was so much fun to listen to them talking about how they affected people.

Overall, children laugh a lot more than adults do. I've read studies that say adults laugh only fifteen or so times a day. I consider myself a relatively happy individual, and I don't think I laugh even nearly that much. Maybe when I'm hanging out with a group of family or friends, but I don't do that on a daily basis. I laughed aloud about an hour ago, and the sound actually surprised me. I find that sad. Come on, people; make me laugh!

Being happy makes you smile, and smiling makes you happier. Try it. I command you to smile right now! If you're unhappy, there's no point in punishing yourself by staying that way.

We put so much responsibility on ourselves to work and take life seriously. Why? Let's have more fun! Think about how much happier the world would be if we took time to make sure we laughed. We should enjoy ourselves. How can you go about making sure you laugh?

I'm not talking about laughing at someone else's expense, whether or not they're in the vicinity. We need to raise vibrations all around—not raise some while depleting others. Keep it simple. There's no good in being counterproductive, and energy is powerful!

Laughter will help your vibrations rise and help you become more spiritual. Since laughter is contagious, you'll raise someone else's spirits in the process.

Laughter doesn't have to be about *being* joyful—it can be about *creating* joy.

Laughter yoga is about creating joy, and it is a real thing. Dr. Madan Kataria is the founder of the School of Laughter Yoga.

On one hand, it's sad that we've let ourselves be so miserable that we can't find time to laugh on a regular basis. On the other hand, it's pretty cool that enough people dedicate their lives to making people happy that such a form of yoga actually exists.

Laughter yoga combines laughter exercises with yogic breathing. Laughter yoga works because motion creates emotion. It's based on the idea that laughter is already within you—you just need to tap it to get it out.

You truly don't need anything funny to get the benefits of laughter. Your body and mind do not differentiate between fake laughter and real laughter; you get the same benefits either way. Besides, if you try it, you'll find that fake laughter usually turns into real laughter. It's silly, but we need silliness, playfulness, and endorphin rushes. And while the mind might think it's silly, and you might be embarrassed, the body will do what you tell it to do. The benefits of the mind will follow.

In laughter yoga, there are experiences of laughing simply to laugh. There are also some funny exercises to help you laugh. Some exercises involve movement, and some involve a little bit of interaction. They're all really simple. You can stand, move around, or sit in one place for the entire time, hardly moving at all.

One of the exercises in laughter yoga involves clapping to create stimulation for your acupressure points on your hands. The one called mental floss helps you laugh your mind clear of mucky thoughts.

Laughing really is like medicine without the negative side effects. Laughing is fun, and it makes you feel lighter. Your problems will be taken care of, and your heart can practically lift up to heaven. The sound of your laughter makes the divine beings very happy! You don't have to leave laughter to chance. Wouldn't you like to be your own guru of giggling?

You can choose laughter or any other form of sound healing to match your vibrations with the happiness that surrounds you if you're open to it. Start with the sounds you appreciate now—and be open to new sounds you find uplifting as you journey on.

Playtime!
Mantra Mumblin'

Make Your Own Whale Sounds

Write a goal of yours in a positive, two-to-seven-word statement.

_____

_____

Rearrange the main letter sounds from each word to make it work for you as a mantra that you can sing all day long.

_____

_____

When discovering my mantra, I wrote: "I need to let go. God will open the doors. I will walk through them and end up where I should go or must go." (I used more than seven words, and you can, too.)

I underlined *God, doors, must,* and *going.* I changed the order to must, go, God, door. That turned into mu-go-ga-doh. To make it simpler and easier to remember, I changed it to God's door, and from there to go-doh.

Now, when I'm searching for direction, I can sing "go-doh" to myself. I remember that I don't have to worry about where I go. Often, I just say, "God's doors" to myself as a reminder when I'm trying to make a decision.

Be careful not to place pressure on yourself to cause a change. Chant your mantra with nonattachment—and the change will come.

-Or-

Make up a song and keep singing it throughout the day. You can sing the same song for days on end or make a new one each day. Make sure it's positive and uplifting to you.

Bang, Bang on the Bowls!

Find something that vibrates to bang on (that you won't ruin, of course) and just bang away. Listen to the vibrations and how they change.

Turn It Up, Toots!

Find some good-for-you music to listen to and jam out! Try to keep your mind on the song, the lyrics, the rhythm, the instruments, and all the other components of the song until the song is over.

Sidesplitting Laughs

Make one person laugh today, two tomorrow, and three the next day. Try to make it up to ten. For bonus points, take notes on how you made people laugh.

_____

_____

_____

_____

_____

-Or-

Make every single person you meet today laugh at least once. (At least try—you can't guarantee they'll think you're funny.) Make sure your ways of making people laugh are actually funny and not hurtful.

-Or-

Simply smile. When you're sitting, working, or whatever, notice what your facial muscles are doing and relax them or turn them into a smile. With practice, you'll notice you scowl a lot more than you realize. Scowls give you wrinkles—don't give yourself wrinkles!

-Or-

Keep a funny journal in a little notebook. Keep it close. Write about funny things that happen or that you hear. Keep it nice so that negativity doesn't creep into the fun. Look at the list every time you want to get your giggle on.

Reiki, Cracks, Acu Taps

Imagine the big guy in the sky sending you healing vibes with his hands. Imagine your spirit becoming lighter because someone put a special energy around you. Imagine being able to put your hands on someone to heal their injury.

If this sounds good to you, Reiki is the spiritual healing energy you're looking for.

Rei means *universal*, and *Ki* means *energy*. Therefore, Reiki is universal energy. It's pronounced ray-key like a ray of sunshine and a key that opens doors.

The Bible says that we all have healing capabilities. Why don't people talk about that more?

Even so, while Reiki is spiritual in nature, it is not a religion. There is not even anything you need to believe in order to allow it to help heal you!

Reiki has the power to return what it touches to healthy functioning in mind, body and spirit. It's based on healing the life energy that flows through you. When your life energy is low, you feel negativity, pain and stress that turn into sickness. When it's high, you're happy and healthy.

Reiki energy is drawn to any negative energy and works to replace that negative energy with positive energy, therefore breaking up energy blockages and replacing the space with free-flowing, healthy energy that keeps on healing as it flows.

If you hear the story of how Usui Reiki Ryoho was brought to us, you might feel like it was literally passed down from heaven to humans. Mikao Usui-Sensei went to a mountaintop in 1922 in search of answers to fill his soul. On the twenty-first day, he felt a powerful energy over his head and suddenly felt spiritually awakened. In his excitement, he ran down the mountain, tripped, and hurt his toe.

When he reached down and grabbed his toe, he felt a new, powerful healing energy flowing through him. He watched his toe healing right in front of his eyes! In amazement, he ran to put his hands on his family members and watched their ailments heal up as well. Eventually, he was able to come up with a way to pass his healing energy onto others—and that's how we still have it around today.

In 1939, Semyon Kirlian accidently discovered a way to capture, on film, the electromagnetic energy fields that all living things give off. Kirlian photographs show auras and prove that our energy fields change shape, size, and colors to match our emotions. Reiki energy shows up in Kirlian photography as pure, bright, white, light energy in the practitioner's hand.

Do you have easy access to Kirlian photography? No? Do you have a tea bag? With the use of a tea bag or other pendulum, you can see how the energy moves without Kirlian photography. You can make a pendulum by tying string around a small object. Hold the pendulum in front of your stomach, heart, throat or head. If you're patient and still, soon you'll be able to watch it move. If you get a treatment or attunement, you'll be able to watch it move even faster since healthy energy moves rapidly.

In 1988, William Lee Rand founded the International Center for Reiki Training (at the time, it was called the Center for Spiritual Development). He trains people to become Reiki practitioners and trainers. In 2010, he put together the Reiki Membership Association (the RMA), which provides professional recognition for members. It gives people who want treatments contact information of practitioners and teachers in their area. The RMA also offers insurance and printable brochures for practitioners and teachers.

If you become a Reiki practitioner at level 1, you can send the energy to yourself and others anytime for physical pain, mental strain, and spiritual healing, as well as to things like plants and to situations in life. This certification is called a Level 1 Attunement.

If you were to go onto to level 2 of certification, it would be called a Reiki Level 2 Attunement, and you would receive symbols for more powerfully reaching specific ailments, for example, emotional and mental addictions, as well as a symbol for performing distant Reiki.

Having the symbol for performing distant Reiki means someone who's not even near you can receive the energy. You could use the distant symbol to send energy to protect your house when you're not home or protect your children when you're not with them. You can send it out into the future, say for a class presentation you're nervous about, or you can send it out into the universe with a little prayer that anyone who needs it will receive it.

If you go on and become a Reiki Master, you can teach, train, and certify others with Reiki attunements to be practitioners.

Reiki is not something you have to study in order to be able to administer. Rather, it's an attunement you receive like a gift as long as you're willing to receive it.

The attunement opens your palm chakras, which is how you will be able to send the energy to yourself and others. You'd be able to see the energy coming from your palm with a pendulum.

Biomagnetic fields of healers' hands are much stronger than those of non-healers' hands—about a thousand times stronger than any other field emitted from the body—and are much stronger than sick organs. How does it work? It's a miracle! The body's cells have liquid crystals that generate electric currents that flow through the body. When the currents are coherent, they produce vibrations that radiate out of the body.

Reiki brings coherence to those currents by sending healthy frequencies into sick organs. The organs adjust their frequencies back into the healthy range so the electrical currents are able to flow more productively, and healing takes place.

The theory is that scalar waves are involved in distant healing. These scalar waves, tesla waves, or longitudinal waves are composed of pure zero-point energy and are capable of penetrating any solid object. They can't be blocked or shielded, they travel faster than the speed of light, and they're capable of passing through the earth from one side to another with no loss of field strength. They have the potential to be used as a power source, for communication, for energy and more.

There are a lot of different ways treatments can be administered. There are millions of practitioners in the world, and thousands of hospitals use the energy for their patients, some during surgery.

I often take a few random seconds to secretly send out the energy. If someone's soul wants to accept it, they will benefit from it even if their brain doesn't know it's there. The energy can be beamed, which is how it should be done to treat animals, at least at first, because they're close to the spiritual realm and are sensitive to it. Reiki flows through the hands, feet and eyes. Yes, you can beam it from your eyes!

A client who goes to a practitioner for a treatment or session will usually lie or sit in a comfortable position and relax. Many practitioners have tables that are like massage tables.

Treatment doesn't involve any muscle manipulation. It's given by hand placements that generally include a light touch or hovering of the hands over the eyes, head, neck, torso, knees and feet.

The energy will often feel warm, but depending on the type of healing taking place, it could feel cold. I had my hand, which I felt very warm energy coming from, on a friend's injured shoulder, and she said, "Why are your hands so cold?"

The way the energy was healing her, rather than the temperature of my hand, was causing that sensation. Sometimes blocked energy is melted away or burned up, causing a warm sensation. At other times, it's released, which causes a cold sensation.

The energy travels to treat other areas in addition to where the hands are placed. The mind, body and soul are all affected. The energy might go to your mind to help your thoughts, which will help your body heal.

You don't have to worry about directing the energy to a certain place or telling the practitioner where to direct the energy, because the energy is energy of a higher consciousness and is spiritually guided.

If you want your knee pain to go away, Reiki energy might decide to help you fix a situation in your life that you weren't aware was causing your knee pain. In that case, the pain will go away after the situation is handled accordingly.

Your session would probably last between a half hour and two hours. One hour is generally sufficient. Reiki energy continues to flow through you and heal you for some time after a treatment.

Some types of energy healing can deplete the practitioner's energy, but Reiki does not.

In fact, Reiki can do no harm whatsoever. Even though we now know all of this stuff about energy, much of the healing work of Reiki remains a mystery. It is a spiritual practice, after all.

Now that you know how to get your healing hands on, let's meet the docs who crack you up! I'm just kidding—the chiropractor doesn't really crack your bones. Chiropractors manipulate your bones so that they're in the correct place. When they do this, little air bubbles pop out from the bone and cartilage areas, which might cause a cracking sound. Yes, it can sound a little creepy, but it's such a sweet release. When the placement of your bones is correct, your muscles can work properly and hold less tension and pain.

Are you a knuckle cracker? During my high school years, cracking your knuckles was cool. I didn't know it was eventually going to lead to very sore hands. The soreness led to apprehensiveness about seeing a chiropractor. I thought the temporary relief would eventually lead to long-term pain.

But my body was in a lot of pain, so I gave it a try, and I asked about it while I was there. It turns out that when we're unnecessarily doing it on purpose, we're causing problems by wearing down the cartilage that we need for cushioning between bones, and this leads to arthritis pain. Cartilage is like your bone's pillows. When the pillows wear down, the bones rub together. Ouch!

When the chiropractor adjusts you, on the other hand, he or she is releasing stuck air that needs to be released for proper joint function and bone movement, which leads to your muscles once again being able to work the way they're meant to, which leads to proper alignment and feeling good all around with easier, healthier movements.

It's been more than fifteen years for me, so I know it doesn't lead to the same kind of pain that I still have in my hands.

Chiropractic care is a holistic mode of health because it works with and eliminates problem areas rather than working around them or covering them up with medicines. It brings the body back to working properly in its natural form. Having treatments when there aren't any obvious problems helps maintain good function so that many issues won't repeat or arise in the first place.

Have you heard chiropractic horror stories? I've heard many people say they've tried the chiropractor, but they stopped going because it made their problem worse.

I have a different idea. If you have muscle pain and a chiropractor makes you feel worse, you're just left feeling worse—and that's no way to live! You should find a different chiropractor who can help you better. Different doctors have different ways of doing things. Some might help you, and some might not help you as much. You owe it to yourself to find the one who can help you, because life is so much sweeter when your body moves painlessly.

It's like finding a general practitioner, a yoga class or an ice cream flavor. The world has room for all kinds of general practitioners, yoga teachers and ice cream flavors! You have a slew to choose from and should keep looking until you find the one your body, mind and spirit jive with the most. If you find the right chiropractor for you, you'll feel like you're walking on air and like you could skip or run without stopping. Really, it can be that good. You owe it to yourself—and you deserve it. Go for the chocolate … I mean, the gold.

Now that you're all cracked up, let's point it out with acupressure points. Have you heard of *acupoints, acupressure, acuballs* or *acupuncture*?

Acupoints are points in your body along the meridians, which are the lines where your energy flows. You can apply pressure to certain acupoints to help other parts of your body heal.

There are acupoints all over the body, but they're especially plentiful in the feet, hands and ears.

To learn how some of these points match up to some of your body parts, picture your foot having your full body next to it.

The toes connect with the head.

The balls of the feet connect with your chest, including the lungs, heart and shoulders.

The middle of the foot connects with your mid and lower torso.

The heels connect with the lower part of the body, including the legs.

The inside of the feet under the big toes and down to the top of the heels connects with the spine.

Are you able to visualize how the foot would line up with the body if the body were as small as the foot? Of course, this is just a general visual. You can find much, much more detailed maps of your meridians.

Your hands have similar points.

The thumbs and fingers connect with the head.

The upper part of the palms connects with the chest, including lungs, heart and shoulders.

The mid palms connect with the mid and lower torso.

The wrists connect with the lower part of your body, including the legs.

The outside of the hand between the thumb and the wrist connects with your spine.

Your ears are another spectacular place to massage on a regular basis—you don't need to wait for an ailment to creep up on you—you're better off working to prevent issues.

The outsides of the ears, where they're floppiest, connect with the hands, wrists, elbows, arms and shoulders.

Just inside of the part described above connects with the feet, ankles, knees and legs.

Closer to the mid ear connects with your organs.

The lower parts of the ears connect with the mouth, teeth, jaws, tonsils and eyes.

Acupressure is when you apply pressure to an acupoint. Massaging your feet, hands and ears can bring great benefits to the entire body, face and head, including for help with headaches, toothaches and sinus problems. It's also good for arthritis pain. There are things to be aware of, however, such as not massaging the point between your thumb and forefinger if you're pregnant unless you're trying to deliver, because it can trigger contractions of the uterus. But if you're trying to deliver, voila!

If you get a professional acupressure massage, the technique will vary depending on the type of massage.

Shiatsu therapy uses deep pressure on various points for three to five seconds.

Thai massages stimulate the *qi*, which is healthy energy, using hand movement along with full body stretches and other massage techniques.

During Jin Shin acupressure, extra meridians are involved in the treatment, and two points are gently held minimally for about a minute.

Acuballs are massage balls with points on them. You rub the ball on the acupressure point and heal from there.

Acupuncture is when an acupuncturist puts needles into specific spots. Never put a needle into yourself! You need to have schooling to know the safe spots. The schooling is well worth it, as acupuncture really has a way of getting the healing done.

You can find a private acupuncturist who works with you alone. For less expense, you can go to a community acupuncture place where they have multiple people being treated in the same room at the same time.

In deciding between private sessions and community sessions, you'll find the amount of clothes you remove will be different, so don't worry about that! You might be asked to expose more skin in a private session. At community acupuncture, you leave all your clothes on except your shoes and socks. If you pull up your pant bottoms and roll up your sleeves, they'll have more areas to place the needles. It will most likely be up to you.

Heel up exploring your acu spots! Get it? Heel up? And, heal up! Now that we've pointed everything out, let's tap, tap, tap it out! Doesn't tapping sound like fun?

Tapping, otherwise known as *emotional freedom technique*, or EFT, is another scientifically proven method of curing ailments caused by emotional issues.

Like acupressure, tapping deals with the meridians, which are the energy pathways of the body. EFT is based on the idea that there are two main emotions: fear and love. Everything that's painful roots from fear, and tapping taps out the fear, so to speak, so that it becomes unstuck and you can be free from it.

The process is just what it sounds like it would be: tapping! Use your fingertips. You can use one hand or both for most areas.

Lightly tap, being gentle to your capillaries, multiple times in a row (three light taps will suffice) each place listed. Repeat the list a few times—and repeat the entire process for multiple days in a row for the best benefit. Ten days should suffice, but you're free to do the tapping technique more or less often as you see fit.

Here is where you tap (three light taps on each of the following body parts, in order):

- the outside of one palm
- the top of the head
- the brow, above or between the eyebrows
- the outside of the eye
- under the eye
- under the nose
- under the mouth

- the collarbone
- your torso, underneath the arm

Note the difference in how you feel after tapping—even subtle feelings count a lot more than they seem.

Playtime!
Rockin' Reiki

How would you like to be healed? Daydream on it. Spend a solid ten minutes imagining how your chakras and aura would be affected by a Reiki treatment. This can be a very powerful meditation!

-Or-

Draw what your chakras and aura are like before a Reiki treatment (what they might look like right now). Then draw what they would be like after a Reiki treatment. You can include the white Reiki energy in your drawing.

Crackin' Craze

Draw a picture of a person with crooked bones and the muscles around them. Imagine the person trying to walk around. In a different color, draw where you think the pain would be.

Now draw a person whose bones are all aligned. You don't need the extra color for pain now! Imagine how much better this person feels than your first person.

Crazy Connections

Make a sock person and color-code the acupressure points.

Tap, Tap, Tap

Lightly tap it out and take notes on how you feel afterward as compared to beforehand. Remember that even subtle changes in feelings and thoughts count.

Here is where you tap (three light taps on each of the following body parts, in order):

- the outside of one palm
- the top of the head
- the brow, above or between the eyebrows
- the outside of the eye
- under the eye
- under the nose
- under the mouth
- the collarbone
- your torso, underneath the arm

_____

_____

_____

_____

_____

_____

_____

Hypnotize *This*, Dreamland!

Hypnotism is when a magician points a wand and makes someone space out and do all these crazy things like act like a walrus. Well, maybe that's how it is at the fair, but as far as holistic healing goes, hypnotism is more like a guided meditation. The messages of the hypnotist sink right down into your unconscious mind, so the results could be as entertaining as an act at the fair!

Have you ever used imaginative suggestions to really feel something you wanted to feel? That's hypnotism! Sounds simple, right? When I used my own imaginative suggestions, I was in my car! Hypnotized while driving? That doesn't sound like a great idea, but I didn't even know that was considered hypnotism at the time. I just wanted to feel the happiness that sunshine and Cheetos could give me when I didn't have sunshine or Cheetos.

If you don't feel you have the power to hypnotize yourself, reach out to professionals in your community. You might be amazed at the resources available. You do have the powers within you, but reaching out to others is a wonderful thing. In a one-on-one hypnosis session, you'll most likely be led through a guided meditation that can leave you feeling more relaxed and clear in the mind.

Hypnotism can be about going into a trancelike state. You might feel calm and relaxed but have elevated concentration and be open to suggestions. For now, just start with raising your vibes by concentrating on something that raises your vibes. You can go back to the brain break meditation mini vacations for your hypnosis practice. Use your imagination and see where it takes you!

Hypnosis is fun to experiment with, but something you truly need is sleep. Get enough sleep! Sleep is when you process and rejuvenate. During a normal day, your mind and body are working overtime while your spirit sits quietly waiting. In order to have mind, body and spirit balance, you need to give your spirit time to flourish.

Would it surprise you to find out that people who meditate generally need less sleep than those who don't? They don't need as much because they're already giving themselves some of the relaxing, nourishing quiet time they need.

Studies show phenomenal results about how sleep improves productivity and efficiency to the point that companies such as Google and Nike have sleep pods in their offices. Even if the employees don't actually fall asleep, enough rest provides the benefits of an adequate nap.

During the day, you expend energy. Where does your energy come from? The louder your mind and daily environment are, the more you need sleep to give you the quiet you need. If you go to bed feeling drained of energy, your energy will be restored with better sleep.

When you think of yourself sleeping at night, what does that picture look like? Are you tossing and turning, glancing at the clock, and wondering if you should get up to go to the bathroom one more time? Are you thinking about work?

Stop!

You're not meant to be thinking about tomorrow's problems today. Did you know that? In fact, one reason we have to wait periodically is so we can learn to take our time with life. We would be overwhelmed if we took it all at once. Let tomorrow's business be tomorrow's business.

Insomnia is a habit, and habits can be really hard to break. However, insomnia's not permanent since habits can be broken until they're just vague memories.

Since visualization is so powerful, picture your bedroom right now and think about what color the walls are. During your visualization, even if you don't see the walls, you are thinking about the colors of the walls and the way your room looks. That's a visualization that will work.

A good way to tackle insomnia is to use that visualization practice to picture yourself sleeping peacefully every time you think of your bedroom. Think about crawling under your cozy blanket in your comfortable bed with a smile on your face as you're looking forward to the peaceful time you'll spend with your quiet mind. Use your imagination if you have to and keep the picture of you sleeping peacefully in your head every time you think about your bedroom and every time you think about sleep.

You'll fall asleep more easily if you have your bedroom free of anything that doesn't pertain to sleep and love. Settling into a room that only pertains to sleep and love sends your body, mind and spirit signals that it's time to rest. And when you are actually trying to sleep, do your best to make yourself comfortable once and stay put, keeping your eyes closed and your thoughts pleasant and simple.

Make yourself have pleasant thoughts that will help you drift into sweet dreams. It will take time and practice, but it will work. Since you always get more of what you focus on, you might as well make it pleasant! The quiet mind allows the soul to emerge and the spirit to lead the way.

You also need a comfortable bed! That means something different to different people, but find what makes you comfortable for your whole night's sleep. If your bed's uncomfortable and for whatever reason you can't get a different one, find a simpler way to make it more comfortable. You might benefit from a foam mattress pad. Go to a sleep store and ask for suggestions based on your specific issues.

Temperature and lighting make a huge difference, too. Your best bet is to be comfortably warm in bed with the air in the room somewhat cool. Being too hot will keep your energy up with sweat production. Some people like their feet cooler. If that's you, stick your feet out from the blanket. Be sure you have enough blankets for the middle of the night when it gets cooler.

You might like a light on for when you get up, but your sleeping self likes the dark better. Your body's natural cycle is to be awake when it's light and asleep when it's dark. You will slip into a better routine if you follow your body's natural way.

Turn off the TV! It's best not to have a TV in your bedroom at all, but at the very least, keep it off during sleep time. Computers and phones need to be off, too. If you insist on keeping your phone in your room for safety measures, can you keep it turned off—or at least have the screen facing down and the volume all the way off? It's important to keep distractions out. Otherwise, you might as well be at work and in full swing.

The hour before bed should be screen-free time because the bright lights stimulate your brain and make it difficult to turn your mind down to quiet.

Eating during the last few hours before bed also hinders good sleep because digestion takes energy and keeps you more alert.

While you're trying to sleep through the night, get out of the habit of looking at the time, no matter what, before the alarm goes off. This can be a difficult habit to get into, but checking the time stimulates your brain and makes it even more difficult to sleep. Trust that the alarm, or sunshine, will wake you up. You owe it to yourself to rest peacefully without worrying about the time.

To add to all these new, wonderful habits, here's a horrid one that might make you absolutely miserable. If unpleasant thoughts linger and keep you awake in the wee hours of the morning, such as your to-do list, situations you can't control, or conversations you'd like to have with someone, get out of bed. It sounds miserable, but you would be retraining your brain to use your bed for sleeping rather than for thinking.

It's no joke! Try it. When you're out of bed early because of this, you can start your morning routine, but if you plan on trying to sleep again, stay away from the bright screens and all the other things that stimulate your brain.

It might take a few weeks to start working, but it's a perfect way to send your brain the message that it won't have any chance to sleep if it doesn't become still. Soon enough, the deeper, more pleasant sleep will come because the need for adequate sleep will win.

I put myself through this painstaking experiment, and it worked. I would be awake stewing about everything about work that bothered me. Things seemed even worse than they were during the day. I started getting out of bed because I was so sick of spending my nighttime thinking about work problems.

When I got up, even though I was tired, I was able to think about other things around me like my dog and my other favorite things. Even thinking about doing the dishes was a relief from the stressful thoughts.

After a few weeks, when I was super overtired, I began to sleep soundly. It was easier to think about sleeping on heavenly clouds and other spiritually pleasant things. It was glorious. Give it a shot. You'll get a lot of bonus dreamtime, and dreamland is the place to be!

Dreamland is your soul's place and time to learn what you're not learning during the day.

Are you one of those people who don't dream? You do! You just don't remember the dreams. According to sleep studies, we all dream, but the memories of the dreams can be elusive.

There are experiments to become better at dream recall.

Make it a rule not to think about your to-do list or anything in your life that causes you stress in your bedroom at all. What a load off! If you get into this habit, it won't be long before you can explore different angles and see situations more clearly.

You can take the power of your brain and train it with the simple habit of, upon first awaking, thinking about what happened last in your memory. Dwell on those details. Reach for the pen and notebook on your bedside table and jot down every little detail about your dream—even if it seems silly or unimportant. Those seemingly silly details will pile up into patterns and more meaning if you keep at it. You'll soon be able to start putting the pieces together. Make it a rule to not think about anything other than your night's sleep until you've finished jotting down your dreams.

In order to figure out what your dreams are trying to do for you, listen to your intuition. You can buy a dream interpretation book to help you figure out the symbolism and possible themes, but from there, you have to put the pieces together for yourself.

The more you pay attention to your dreams, the more peaceful they'll become. That's because your sleep guides are having an easier time getting through to you! Hindsight is twenty-twenty, so it might take a while before you see how things had been aligning the whole time.

Paying attention to your dreams can be fun, and it beats thinking about your daily tasks right when you wake up. And you never have to worry because those daily tasks will force their way into your brain when it's time for them. You'll start to see how your dreams, however boring or wild, relate to your waking life. From there, you'll be able to learn and grow. Sometimes you might not see how they relate, and that's okay because you don't have to know how they relate. It's more about the experience.

Your soul knows what your dreams mean. You can count on that. It's nice when the brain knows too, and that's what your dream journal is for.

Paying attention to your dreams isn't fun if your dreams are scary. We all have scary dreams at some point in our lives, but scary dreams are usually your soul's way of having you experience awful situations so that you learn the lessons without having to experience the situations in your waking life. Isn't that where you'd rather experience them?

Many times, when a person has a scary dream, they worry that it's a premonition dream. There are such things as premonition dreams, but for most of us, that's not the case.

Bad dreams can also be caused from worry, guilt, anger and other types of fear. The dream might be hinting to you to figure out your negative feelings so you can turn them around. When you have a dream involving a very strong negative emotion, it's a sign that you have pent-up emotions. You should resolve whatever situation in your waking life is causing that emotion.

Astral travel dreams can take you back home to heaven where your soul truly feels at peace and whole. You can travel back home as often as you like. Just think of what it might be like as you fall asleep, and see what kind of journey you go on. You can explore answers and receive guidance from enlightened beings that want to help you.

After you get used to remembering your dreams, you'll eventually be able to start controlling your dreams! Once you figure that out, be sure to make them adventuresome and nurturing!

Experience more dreaming, sleeping, and hypnotism to explore the more awesome reality beyond your earthly illusions. You'll become more fulfilled in so many different ways, and you'll be glad you put forth the effort. It's like taking mini vacations that are healing and nourishing each day, and getting back to the basics will help you live your best life.

Playtime!
Happy Hypnotist

Use your imagination to pretend. Give yourself five minutes or so to really feel each of these things:

1. Someone who loves you is hugging you.
2. Something funny is making you laugh.
3. You are dancing to your favorite music.
4. Your dreams are all coming true.
5. The sun is coming out and shining down on you.

Serious Sleep

At least one hour before bed …

- Turn off your TV!
- Turn off your games!
- Turn off your phone!
- Turn off your computer!

The lights affect your eyes and make it difficult for your brain to shut down. Give yourself a good night's sleep every night and see how much better you feel.

-Or-

Get into the habit of a daily afternoon nap. Set a timer for somewhere between ten and thirty minutes.

Dreamland—Where It Gets Real

Keep a dream journal by keeping a small notebook and a pen next to your bed. When you wake up, focus on what was just happening instead of what will happen once you get up.

Every once in a while, read your dreams back. You'll notice how much weirder they seem once you're wide-awake—but you'll also see how they connect to your real life and how you can let your dreams help you.

Spiritual Toys

Why do children play with rocks? Is it just because they don't have enough toys? Hardly! Kids are attracted to rocks because rocks are filled with good earth energy. Kids can sense this positive energy.

Since crystals are found in an active part of the earth's crust, they also hold earth energy. The atoms of all crystals are more active than other solid objects. The vibrational energy of rocks and crystals helps heal living things and situations because the energy contains unique electromagnetic charges that affect the vibrational energies of people and things in their path.

Some people say that crystals are partially from earth and partially from heaven.

Did you know that our bodies have liquid crystals? These liquid crystals flow through our bodies and generate electric currents. Even with liquid crystals, as we get older, we become less sensitive to the energies of other living things. However, you can use the energies of other crystals to help heal your own.

We don't have a lot of scientific proof of this yet, but what's the harm in trying? It makes total sense, and if nothing else, it can be fun to be an adult with a toy. To work on your healing using crystals, you have various options. You can place a chakra-colored crystal on each chakra and let them rest for fifteen or twenty minutes. You would use violet for the crown, indigo for the brow, blue for the throat, green for the heart, yellow for the solar plexus, orange for the sacral area, and red for the root. It goes in the same order as the colors of the rainbow.

If you only have one crystal, you can leave it on each chakra for three minutes per chakra. Start at the head and do the feet last so that you or the person you're treating is grounded when the session is over.

You could hold crystals close to the ailment or around the chakra associated with that body part. Crystals that are especially powerful include jasper, amber, citrine, peridot, jade, agate, aquamarine, moonstone, amethyst and clear quartz. Here are some specific ideas for healing ailments with crystals:

- Jasper helps balance your root chakra and contains oxides of iron with red, yellow, brown and green. It's grounding, so it helps you feel less judgmental and helps you connect with nature's power.
- Amber is a stone that was formed from tree resin and naturally fossilized. It's good for the sacral area since it detoxifies, purifies, and provides a protective shield.
- Citrine is good for your solar plexus, for productivity, and for acquiring success and generosity.
- Peridot is connected to the heart. It was brought up to the earth's surface with volcanoes and earthquakes. It naturally heals emotional, physical, and mental issues, and it brings positive energy. It's also associated with Archangel Raphael.
- Jade is a stone for the heart. It's lucky, so it can help you achieve your goals. It also brings wisdom, courage and tranquility.
- Agate is quartz for your throat chakra. It's known as the earth's rainbow, and because it vibrates at a lower frequency, it strengthens and stabilizes you. It gives self-confidence and courage.
- Aquamarine is good for the throat. It means *water of the sea*, and it helps with clarity and proper communication of your feelings. It helps you explore hidden meanings.
- Moonstone holds the magic of the moon. It's used for the third eye, uncovers hidden truths of your soul and your deep-seated feelings, and helps lead you to your destiny.
- Amethyst is quartz for the crown. It relieves stress, works for spiritual protection and growth, and comforts you when you're sad.
- Clear quartz crystals are for the crown. A lot of scientists are fans of clear quartz for the studies that show positive results. It's like they're living pieces of divine energy that are bringing guidance from the higher realm.
- Lapis lazuli is good for headaches.
- Sunstone is good for sore throats.
- Sodalite is good for digestive issues.
- Rose quartz is good for burns and blisters.
- Rhodonite is good for bites and other skin wounds.
- Malachite is good for inflammation.

- Aventurine purifies your thoughts and helps reduce fear and anxiety.
- Hematite cleans up your blood and charges up will, courage, and personal magnetism.
- Lapis activates the thyroid gland and strengthens the connection to spirit and therefore psychic abilities.
- Obsidian connects your mind and emotions, and it grounds spiritual energy in the physical plane.
- Tourmaline helps you sleep and eliminates fear and negativity.

If you get crystals, you can energetically clean them periodically with dry salt, salt water, smudging or visualization. You can reenergize them with a sun and moon bath by keeping them under the sky for twenty-four hours.

If you decide to go to a crystal therapist, your session details will depend on your practitioner. Crystal therapists don't need certification, so there are no regulations for how to hold a session. Some are registered with professional associations and some are not.

The therapist may ask you for medical history, lifestyle, and other personal situations. Feel free to share what you're comfortable sharing. The more they know, the more they might be able to help you. Your intention for specific healing might affect your healing process just as much. Since the crystal therapist won't be diagnosing you, there's no need to dish out problems you're not comfortable dishing out.

During your session, you might feel energetic changes. Some might feel negative, including a deeper feeling of what ails you in the first place! This seems backward, but it's caused from a toxic release. Just go with it. If it gets intense, your therapist might have suggestions for you. I suggest that you notice your breath, deepen and slow it, and focus on your intention of continuing the healing process.

Have fun playing with your crystals! There's no right or wrong, really, with allowing crystals to heal you. Just having them nearby can influence your energies, and you can play however you like.

You can connect them to a string or chain to make a pendulum! Pendulums are any objects hanging from a string or chain. If you're using a crystal, your pendulum will be especially sensitive to the surrounding energies, but you can tie a paper clip or a pencil to a string. You could also use a tea bag that is already connected to a string.

It's that simple! Just hold the end and suspend the object in midair. Be patient. Does it move at all? It might start to jiggle. When the pendulum is first syncing up with the energy surrounding it, it might shake slightly. It will jiggle when it's "thinking" or beginning to respond to the energy. If you're patient, you'll most likely see more movement. It will begin to move from side to side or in clockwise or counterclockwise circles.

You can intend that the pendulum heals your energy blockages or ask questions and get advice. Does it sound crazy to get advice from a pendulum? You must believe by now that everything is made up of energy. Scientists have been telling us that for a long time. Even solids aren't totally solid since their particles are in constant motion with small vibrational movements.

Because the pendulum is heavy, and the string or chain allows movement, the energy surrounding the pendulum affects its movement. You can test the energy of living and nonliving things. If you hold it longer with the intention of healing any blockages, the effects happen as it moves more and more freely.

When you ask for healing, the divine spirits hear you and want to send you that healing. When you hold a pendulum and ask for healing, it will move faster. You're seeing the spiritual energy healing your blocked energies.

When you ask for advice or ask a question, your subconscious and beings from the divine—most likely your personal spirit guides—can manipulate the energy around the pendulum to deliver that answer to you.

Tell your pendulum (aka your subconscious or your spirit friend) what you would like a yes answer to look like. For example, a *yes* might show up as a circular movement from the pendulum. Next, tell your pendulum what you would like a no answer to look like. For example, it could be a back-and-forth movement.

You could, instead, ask what a yes answer would look like and what a no answer would look like. Be patient while waiting for the response. You can stop it from swinging with your words or your hands in between questions.

Be sure you're asking yes-or-no questions when you want yes-or-no answers. Ambiguous questions will lead to ambiguous answers.

Be patient. If you're not getting a clear answer, you can try as many times as it takes. Your spirit guide has been waiting your entire life to help you more than he or she has always been able to, and your spirit guide doesn't suffer from the impatience that you probably do, so there are always more opportunities.

One possible reason for not getting a clear answer is that, on some level, deep down in your soul or in your subconscious, you don't really want the answer. If you're putting fear into knowing the answer, you might be causing blocks to receiving clear answers.

Another possible reason for unclear answers is that you might be inadvertently controlling the movement of the pendulum with the energy you're putting out into the atmosphere from your own thoughts and feelings.

Being aware of those possibilities might be enough to curb them from happening, but if not, there is a trick you can try. Close your eyes until the pendulum is doing its thing—and then open your eyes and see what it's doing.

It can help to write down your questions first, so that if you need clarification later, you can look back and maybe see things more clearly.

I once asked the pendulum to circle clockwise to signify a *yes* and counterclockwise to signify a *no*. I asked, "Am I going to get pregnant?" It circled clockwise. I asked, "Am I going to have a boy?" It circled counterclockwise. I asked, "Am I going to have a girl?" It circled counterclockwise. With frustration, I asked, "Am I going to have a baby?" It circled counterclockwise. I tried again until I was too frustrated in my state of unknowing. The next month, I found out I was pregnant. The following month, it turned into a miscarriage.

You can see that the answers seemed confusing, but they were right. Sometimes the truth leaves you heartbroken, so be sure you want the answer you're seeking! The pendulum isn't to blame, and the spirit guides that are moving your pendulum aren't to blame, and you aren't to blame! Life is meant to hold certain difficulties for each of us—that's why we're here.

Guidance can come from nearly anywhere if you send the intention. Tarot cards can be used for fun in some of the same ways. They can be used for healing and answering questions. Tarot cards don't need to be handed out for you by a psychic. You can use them on your own, not being psychic, to seek signs or ask for simple advice before making decisions.

It's not as much of a mystery as some people seem to think. Tarot cards have pictures on them and usually come with descriptions of what each one stands for. From there, you can apply meanings to your life situations and see if you can draw advice or guidance from them. The meanings of the cards can be interpreted in many different ways and can lead to positive guidance.

When I was confused and nervous about finding a new career, tarot cards were read to me. The tarot card reader said that the first card would represent my main path in life, the second would represent where I had been recently, the third would represent where I was at the present time, the fourth would represent where I'd be going in the future, and the fifth card would represent what I would need to get there. As he drew the cards, he said they were giving him goose bumps. The first, third and fifth were power cards.

The first card was a picture of a female's face with white light emanating from her—universe. The tarot card reader said my life path has to do with the universe—possibilities could include school, yoga for kids, spiritual healing, and energy healing.

The second card, where I've been recently, was trapped in fear. I knew firsthand that it was true! I was feeling so trapped in fear from searching for answers on my own and feeling like I wasn't getting anywhere.

The next power card, where I was at the moment, was hope. The reader said it was the perfect time to let go with humor. He told me that the answers would come flooding in. He said it was telling me I needed to let go and let God, and listen to what comes from the spirit world through self-healing and self-care for my own health and spirituality.

The fourth card, where I'd be going in the future, was positive forward movement. It was a picture of a sailboat heading into the sun.

The last power card was balance. That would be what I would need in order for the rest to work out. He told me that I'd have to work on balance. I would have to let go of resentments toward people or situations that I felt had caused my grieving from leaving a career that had previously been fulfilling. He said I should have humor finding my playground. This was all coming from a tarot card reader who didn't know my life story!

The cards were actually chosen by my spirit guides. The spirit guides are constantly trying to give you signs. If you seek them out, they can help you more easily. Considering that I wasn't even looking for tarot guidance before I had the reading, it was definitely helpful in giving me hope, confidence and reassurance in my road ahead.

Don't be afraid of what a tarot reading could do for you. Keep in mind that there are various interpretations of what each card symbolizes. Be sure to choose a deck that you like and vibe with, and if a card doesn't make sense to you, look up different meanings for that card to see if any make more sense. Even the death card doesn't usually mean literal death. It means change, like the end of a situation that has been taking up much of your life.

Does any of this seem magical to you? That you just think of a situation or question in your life, pick up a card, read the description of what it symbolizes, and formulate or intuit an answer from there?

Do you believe in magic? Do it! Do it! Believe in magic! Life is grand if you're willing to see the magic in it all.

Or, let life be boring. It's totally up to you.

Whether you believe in magic at this point in your life or not, once you let magic become real for you, everything else seems wondrously unreal. Your problems and fears become more unreal because, considering you're a spiritual being in a temporary physical body, they are.

Different people talk about the same things in different ways. Magic is an example of this. It's good to realize the similarities while you're searching for the truth. *Magic* is the word a lot of people use for things they can't explain. Spiritual energy, raising vibrations, and healing our energies really are like magic.

Vibrations are at all different levels, but that energy is very real even though you can't see it. Raising your vibrations, which raises your consciousness, can help you get in touch with the magical energy that surrounds you.

We can't really explain everything that happens spiritually or everything we're able to do with our spiritual powers, but they are magically powerful!

Plus, there are so many spiritual helpers out there that of course things that seem magical can happen.

Get creative and have fun with it. Life can always get better!

If you look for advice in horoscopes, you might find they can seem a bit magical, too. Reading horoscopes is part of a lot of people's daily routine, even though many people don't believe they hold any weight. Many scientists consider astrology too general to test for evidence.

Do you know where horoscopes come from? Constellations, or groups of stars, radiate wonderfully strong energies. During their rotations, when they're behind the sun, the sun magnifies their energies and sends those energies to earth. Those energies affect us as much as the other energies we're surrounded by.

You can use horoscopes as general advice to lead you to answers or guidance. You don't have to go to any extreme like skipping an audition just because your horoscope said you should find solitude for the day. Instead, you could use the advice as a reminder to be true to yourself by being mindful and leading with your best spiritual self while you rock that audition.

Have fun with horoscopes if they raise your vibrations, and ignore them if they don't do anything for you. You can use them any way you want.

You can find and use number patterns to seek guidance as well. There are lots of theories for recurring number patterns in your life, and one is that they're just coincidence. On the other hand, many psychologists and other professionals say there are no coincidences.

What do you think? Use your intuition when you see number patterns. If you think there's something to it for you, notice what patterns you're seeing and try to connect them to what is happening in your life.

Here is a list of what some spiritual codes signify:

- 111 is a symbol that a spiritual door is opening up for you, so your thoughts will more quickly become things. Keep up your hope and let your fears fly away!
- 222 reassures you that whatever situation you're troubled by will work out on its own, so you should stop worrying about it.

- 333 reminds you that you're being spiritually guided and protected.
- 444 shows you that you're being spiritually guided and that you have an angelic nature. Go, you!
- 555 means the changes you're going through are for your advantage. Instead of resisting them, take them as opportunities to adjust your life to how you want it to be.
- 666 alerts you to focus on healing and balancing your life.
- 777 recognizes you for following divine guidance and helping people around you.
- 888 symbolizes the infinity of energy, which brings balance and abundance. Do you see how the continuous loop of the eight is a symbol for infinity?
- 999 tells you to complete something you've started, like following through on making your dreams come true with no worrying or excuses.
- 142 simply but wondrously means everything's okay.

Don't be afraid of the numbers six or thirteen or any other number—unless you want to be afraid, but it isn't necessary.

When it comes to the reality of number patterns meaning anything, there's something to be said about your personal intention. If you intend or believe that number patterns mean nothing in your life, then they don't have to mean anything. If you want them to mean something to you, you can intend—put the message out into the universe—for them to guide you. You can let your spirit guides or angels know what you want certain numbers to represent and let them use those numbers as signs to guide you when you ask specific questions.

Right now is a great time to let your intuition and your spirit guides help you! Take the time to treat the kid in you to some new toys. Buy some crystals, pendulums, or other magical toys that speak to you and play with them every chance you get. Get some for someone you love as well. Raise vibes! You'll find the connection with your spirit guides and your higher self really seals your heart, mind and soul for a better day.

Playtime!
Ol' Shinies

Buy a quartz crystal. The small ones can be found for a very low price.

-Or-

Buy one crystal for each chakra or rainbow color—red, orange, yellow, green, blue, indigo and violet. You can probably find small ones for less than a dollar or a couple dollars for each.

Just enjoy your crystals for what they are. If nothing else, they connect you to the earth and spirit world at the same time.

Send them requests for healing. Play, play, play—and enjoy!

Pendulum Play

Put a pendulum together. You could tie a pencil, paper clip, rock, crystal or other object to a string. You can even use a shoestring.

Hold it over a solid object like a toy, be patient, and notice what it does. You should see some sort of movement, however slight.

Next, hold it over a rock, plant, or flower, and notice what happens.

Then, hold it over a pet or a child.

Most likely, there is slight movement over the toy, a bit more over the rock, plant or flower, and quite a lot over the pet or child.

Do you see a difference in vibrational energy? Take note of what you see:

_____

_____

Try it again at a different time and see if there's a different result:

_____

_____

-Or-

While sitting or standing, hold the pendulum in front of you. You could also lie down and hold it over your body. Notice how it moves. Does it go from side to side? Clockwise? Counterclockwise?

Hold it in front of your root, at your legs and lower hip area. How does it move?

_____

_____

Next, hold it in front of your sacral area, below the belly button. How does it move?

_____

_____

Hold it in front of your solar plexus, above the belly button. How does it move?

_____

_____

Hold it in front of your heart. How does it move?

_____

_____

Hold it in front of your throat. How does it move?

_____

_____

Hold it in front of your forehead. How does it move?

_____

_____

Hold it over the crown of your head. How does it move?

_____

_____

-Or-

Watch yourself healing right in front of your own eyes. Hold the pendulum at your root. Be patient. Think healthy thoughts and ask that healing energies soak into you at that spot. Watch as it moves more and more. Maybe you'll see the movement switching from side-to-side to circles. Your blockages are becoming unblocked, and your energies are moving more healthfully.

Whenever you're ready to be done, move up through the other chakras, being patient and awed at the power to heal the flow of your energies!

Notice how you're feeling. Do you feel more vibrant? More energetic? More centered?

Write about your experience:

_____

_____

_____

_____

-Or-

Ask your pendulum for good advice. Be sure to set what a yes or no answer would look like, and be certain to ask yes-or-no questions.

What answers are you getting?

_____

_____

_____

_____

Turn Up the Tarot

Get a deck of cards, tarot or not. If they're tarot, you have it made.

If not, that's okay, too. Assign each card to one of the following: new beginnings, awareness, intuition, creativity, authority, wisdom, harmony, winning, power, solitude, destiny, balance, sacrifice, change, patience, temptation, disruption, hope, shadow, light, truth, universe, and anything else you choose.

Then, when you ask a question or want to receive advice, receive the advice in the way that works for you.

Use Your Magic Wand—You're the Magician!

Have you ever heard that you can actually control time? That's because time is fluid—you can mess with it.

Visualize yourself being on time or early even when the clock makes you think you're going to be late.

How did it work?

_____

_____

Imagine a meeting going very well and moving quickly—even when you fear it will go all sorts of wrong and take forever.

How did it work?

_____

_____

Hazy Horoscopes

Just for fun, find a horoscope that matches your day, and use that same source for your horoscope each day. See how accurate it is. There are many different publishers of horoscopes, and they're all different. If one doesn't seem to connect to your life, keep searching.

Nosy Numbers

Pay attention to numbers you see—maybe even take note of them so you can notice whether patterns are repeating for you. Write down how the numbers connect with what is going on in your life right now. It might take some time to see patterns and make those connections.

Write the number pattern you see:

_____

_____

Write what is happening in your life right now:

_____

_____

Possible connections:

_____

_____

On another day, write what number pattern you see:

_____

_____

Write what is happening in your life right now:

_____

_____

Possible connections:

_____

_____

And on another day, write the number pattern you see:

_____

_____

Write what is happening in your life right now:

_____

_____

Possible connections:

_____

_____

Now and Zen

You deserve to have stuff, but you don't need more than you need. Be careful that you're not finding your identity in material things. Is it important to have a fancy car, a big house, stylish clothes, or popular-at-the-time items that you don't even really want? Do you have so much money tied up in your stuff that you're "too broke" for much else?

Be careful that material things don't become more important to you than the actual important things like love, the people around you, and your connection with yourself and the divine. If you look more closely, you might find that you're finding part of your identity in *things*. Instead, find your entire identity within your soul and your divinity.

Studies show that people become more materialistic around fancy stores; a person on crutches is more likely to receive an offer of help in a random neighborhood than in front of a high-priced retail store. Why is that? Apparently, something about the materialistic atmosphere makes people more materialistic and less kind.

People are more affected by their surroundings than they realize. Try not to be that person who behaves differently depending on where you are, and you'll save yourself from a world of struggles.

Your specific struggles are there for a reason, but they don't have to remain in your life. If you currently struggle with money, consider whether having a lot of money would draw your attention away from your search for the truth. A lot of people who have it all going for them materially don't find a need to reach out spiritually. During which situations in life do you search most for answers?

Many people pray or search for answers more during difficult times than when life is easy. If that's you, decide to reach out spiritually even during easy times. You're meant to seek truth about your own spirituality. Life circumstances will often shape around how you're doing with your life's purpose. In other words, life just might get easier for you as you continue to seek out spiritual truths!

It's important to be your true self where you are in the *now*.

You are where you are, after all. Duh! But are you really? Or are you thinking about material things, the past, or the future instead of what's happening now? Be in the now—that's a Zen way to live.

Reflecting on the past can help with now and in the future, and making plans for your future can give you something to work toward. However, living in the past is no good. The past is gone. You don't have to deal with it anymore. Living in the future is no good because tomorrow is meant to be for tomorrow.

How would you rather live your life? Being happy once you get what you want? Being happy now while you're still on your way to getting it? Being happy living your life right now whether you end up getting it or not? It's your choice!

Think about the way you think. Do you see that you have a certain way of seeing things that limits you?

Your thoughts become your words.

Your words become your behaviors.

Your behaviors become your habits.

Your habits become your values.

Your values become your destiny.

Think again about the way you think. Do you want that to become your destiny? Now, dump that limiting way of thinking for new waves of happiness.

Most of our fears never actually happen, and worrying won't stop something from happening anyway. It's like a rocking chair—you keep going and going but never get anywhere. If you refuse to worry, you save energy for other parts of life.

Do you have a mind that analyzes a lot? Overanalyzing is when you analyze to the point of pointlessness. It's exhausting! Try not to add to what is actually happening during any situation, including possible hidden meanings or undue analysis. Take it as a source of relief that overanalyzing doesn't make anything better. Give yourself permission to stop.

Negative thinking and bad feelings happen by human nature—so don't be too hard on yourself. Have your thoughts. Just take care to acknowledge them so they can pass. The freedom you get from leading more of a Zen life will be worth it!

Do you want to live a Zen life? One practice is to stop working so hard. Wouldn't that take a burden off your shoulders? Zen is a state of centeredness and being exactly who you are in the here and now. It's doing anything you do with a particular concentration, calmness and simplicity of mind in a way that brings enlightenment and happiness.

Our days are divided into days and nights and hours and minutes so we don't have to experience all of the hardships at once. Be happy about that, and let that encourage you to live in the now. You're meant to experience experiences when, and only when, you actually experience them. Repeating mistakes and other troubles in your head causes you to experience them over and over again.

The same goes for feelings. See feelings for what they are. They are feelings—nothing more and nothing less. When you're done feeling them for a short time, you have the choice to hold on to them or let them go. You're only meant to feel them for a short time. Your soul will learn what it needs to learn—even if you let them go soon.

Do you ever feel overwhelmed by your own emotions when you feel like you shouldn't be? Maybe they even flip-flop from one to the other without warning. Do they ever get in your way? Do they make you behave in ways you regret or make you say things you wish you could take back?

Humans are a lot more emotional than we have to be. In the spiritual world, there are emotions, but they aren't as extreme, and they aren't negative. Negative emotions are of this world, and they are seriously unnecessary. That doesn't mean we can or should just turn into unemotional beings. Even if they're unnecessary, we have them. Expressing them is necessary for moving on and for our health.

Think about situations in life that are important enough to deeply explore the emotions of:

- clueing in to how others feel
- evaluating relationships
- falling in love
- a breakup
- the death of someone you love

Add your own:

_____

_____

_____

Now, think about your emotions that do not entail life-altering situations. Let them go or change them. You have that power.

Are you bored? Entertain yourself. You can turn whatever you're doing into a fun song: Here I go a-walking along … thinking about my day … Here I go a-walking along … come to me what may.

People sing to babies to make them happy—so sing to *you* to make *you* happy! You have the power to make sad energy happy. Have you ever seen a sad dog? He's happy as soon as you pay attention to him. You can change to being happy that quickly, too.

Any sort of anger you have toward another person hurts you more than it hurts that person. It certainly doesn't make you feel better, and you're not making the situation better by being angry.

When you get irritated, let it go. I know it's easier said than done, but it's a practice. Irritation doesn't do you any good unless it's there to help you practice a lesson such as patience.

Anger and irritation come from impatience. Patience is a major life lesson to learn and practice. With all the difficult times, the parts of your chart that you don't know yet, and the magnitude of your emotions, patience can really be key to keeping your cool and your vibes intact.

While teaching middle school students, I figured out the first year that I was going to have to practice patience with my reactions. When I began teaching yoga, I realized I would have to practice patience physically. They were two very different challenges, but practicing patience made a big difference both times.

Have you ever noticed how the more hectic life becomes, the more you lose or drop things? Zen stops that cycle because the opposite is also true: the calmer you become, the steadier you become. Good habits to living a Zen life include doing only one thing at a time, and doing it slowly, deliberately and thoroughly.

"But I don't have time."

Make the time! It's up to you to use your time to do things that are good for you. Do things you enjoy. Make time to sit quietly and meditate. Tune in to your intuition many times throughout the day—as often as you think of it.

Learn to accept and appreciate things for how they are. Act as though whatever happens to you is the best thing that could possibly happen. It may sound absurd or impossible for a lot of life's situations, but if you get into this habit, you'll find that your situations result in your inner happiness more often.

Let day-to-day tasks like cleaning become a form of meditation. Can you see how changing your thoughts could change the whole chore? There is a Zen saying that goes like this: "Before enlightenment, there is chopping wood and carrying water, and after enlightenment, there is chopping wood and carrying water." In other words, the chores will be there no matter what!

You choose whether the enjoyment is there as you take care of tedious business. Can you enjoy chopping wood and carrying water? Most likely you don't have to, but most of us do have to clean the house, pay bills, and run errands. What if you can enjoy those things? You can! You don't have to change the outside world in order to change the way you feel about it and handle it.

I started pretending like that when I first bought a house. Cleaning and yard work weren't fun, but I wanted to stop dreading it. When it was time to do dishes, I would purposefully think about how fun it was to have such colorful dishes. It occurred to me how much I love to have a clean house as I cleaned. When I paid the bills, I thought about how I loved to spend money on bills—no, not really. Actually, I thought about how lucky and thankful I was that I had a job and enough money to pay bills. When I ran errands, I tried to think about the people I might meet along the way. Think of it as a vacation for the brain to stop thinking about work!

If you have a messy storage room, do you have to straighten it up? What do you think the Zen answer would be? If the messiness bothers you, clean and organize it. If it doesn't bother you, there's no reason to worry about it!

Many parts of life, including ambition, can be Zen-like or un-Zen-like. Ambition to improve yourself and your life is great, but ambition to get ahead of others at the expense of compassion is un-Zen-like.

A guru once asked his student a very deep and meaningful question. Do you want to know what the student answered? The student answered, "I don't care." Can you guess how the guru responded? He said that was the perfect answer! It was kind of like saying, "I will be happy no matter what." That's a Zen life.

Other ways to become more Zen-like are to live simply and to remember that the universe doesn't make mistakes. You can smile with your whole being, including your face, whether you're just completing regular tasks or have a huge change sweeping into your life. You never know when things will change!

It's only natural that things change. Change is one of the most difficult things to face because we get comfortable with where we are, but refusing to change is like holding on to what was meant for the past instead of growing forward into what's meant for now.

What are some ways you can embrace change? Can you imagine what life would be like if everything always stayed the same? It would be so weird! Even though we know that is true, change is difficult, especially when it comes unexpectedly. The only way to make sense out of unexpected change is to go with it in a way that flows. Resisting it won't work. Flowing with it will help it turn out in the best way possible for you—even if you don't see it at the time. In fact, the way you accept or resist change will often influence how other things in your life unfold.

When you feel close to your truth, you find it easier to be happy during difficult times. If you're in the habit of accepting things as they are, you won't be as surprised by unexpected changes that come up.

Have you noticed how everyone has problems, but your problems are so different than the problems other people face? You're here on earth to become stronger. Sometimes you will be struck at your weakest points. The weakest points are what need strengthening. It makes sense, really, even though it's probably not what you want to hear. If you get into a habit of accepting life's challenges, life will flow more easily.

Believing that the universe is alive and aware of you at your essence can help you understand why life happens the way it does. You are cared for and loved by the universe. You are one with it. We all are. Go be Zen-like, for your own sake.

Who's more Zen-like in the following scenarios?

Janie was in a traffic jam because there was an accident up ahead. Her thought process went something like this: She'd be late for work; her coworkers would think she was a slacker, and her bosses would think she was unreliable. She would never get a promotion, and her future would be bleak at best. At the very least, everything would go downhill from there for the rest of the day. Everything bad happens to Janie! And when she steps into work, don't people know it! She's shaking off her bad energy all over the place, and no one wants to be around her.

Manuel was in a traffic jam because there was an accident up ahead. His thought process went something like this: *Hopefully the people involved are okay, the authorities will guide the traffic around as soon as possible, and everyone at work will understand if I'm late.* In the meantime, Manuel appreciates that he gets to spend some extra time in the peace of his own thoughts and with good music on the radio. He knows he can't do anything to change the traffic jam; his work will still be there for him when he gets there, and he can make up anything he missed by taking whatever action is needed. It will all work out for the best, no matter what, even if it doesn't seem like it. When Manuel finally gets to work, everyone is so happy he's there. His positive energy is shaking off all over the place. Manuel's life is a happy one, for sure.

Considering these scenarios, who would you say applies fear to life situations? Janie does, right? Who applies hope to life situations? Manuel. If you had to switch lives with one of these people, who would you rather be? You'd rather be Manuel, right? I hope so!

For your own sake, as well as for everyone else's sake, don't be a downer. Fear is natural and more common than necessary, and that is an understatement. Don't berate yourself for fear, but do change your habits for your own good.

Think about a situation happening in your life.

Now think about the way you feel about it.

Is it a positive feeling or a negative feeling?

If it's positive, it's a feeling of hope.

If it's negative, it's a feeling of fear. If it's fear, it's an illusion! Isn't that crazy to think about? Humans made up fear. We have learned it, and we've conditioned ourselves to it.

If you don't think that fear could possibly be an illusion, remember all the things you've feared at one time or another. How many of them ended up happening? Pretend that fear is an illusion. How does that make you feel? You can crawl out of the hole of fear.

Worry, remorse, guilt, blame, anger, agitation, sadness, shame, sorrow, despair, anxiety, angst, dread, doubt, panic, suspicion, cowardice, fright, and all other ugly emotions come from some sort of fear. They cause ugliness, irritability, jumpiness, losing your temper, and missing opportunities.

Fears and worries do not cause you to be able to control your future. Fear is an illusion, but it causes absolute real pain and agony. Isn't it a shame that something we make up in our own heads causes such real pain? If you know you shouldn't let something bother you, so you suppress your worries, they will show up in your body as physical pain.

Think of your current situations that are causing some type of fear. Consider any chronic physical pain you have. Chronic pain is any pain that repeats or never seems to totally go away. It could be that your fear over life situations is causing the pain. The body, mind and spirit are connected. The mind causing physical pain is more relevant than our brains realize.

One man, for example, went to a Reiki practitioner for shoulder pain that wouldn't go away. It didn't seem to work on his shoulder, but his relationship with his mother-in-law began to improve. Can you guess what happened after the relationship improved? Yes, that's right—his shoulder pain decreased until it was gone. The fear he had, whether it was in the form of anger, anxiety or other angst, was causing physical pain, and it wouldn't go away until the situation that was causing his pain subsided.

Get used to noticing your fears of all shapes and sizes. It's worth a try to hope your pain away, but connecting the pain to the situation that's causing it can help even more. Once you find the connection, be one with it rather than trying to separate yourself from it. From there, you can more easily let it go.

Most of our stress comes from wanting to make things happen or wanting to control the way life goes. Since it's not our job to control the world, when we try to control it, it can get stuck in the body as pain.

Forgive yourself for whatever situations you're going through in life—and for causing yourself any fear-based pain. Going forward, try to control your thoughts rather than your situations. If you fear that you're going to get sick, you're thinking sickly thoughts. If you think sickly, you're more likely to become sick. If you hope you keep feeling good and healthy, you're thinking good, healthy thoughts. If you think healthy thoughts, you'll more likely stay healthy.

If your fear is catching the cold that's going around, your hope statement could be: "I hope I keep feeling good and healthy."

Whenever you're thinking about the future or the past, there's no room in your head for now. So, instead of experiencing life, you're just thinking about it. Get back to living it now—and you might enjoy it again.

In every decision you make, you get to decide whether you make it from a place of hope or a place of fear. If an answer comes with love and good feelings, it's the truth. If it comes with fear, it's not.

The only way to go through life is one step at a time, so there is no point to fear the future. When you're anxious, you're focusing on the outside world. Change the direction of your thoughts inward and onto the divine. Rather than trying to anticipate troubles, trust yourself and the divine universe enough to face problems when they come.

Negative experiences are meant to bring you wisdom so that you get to know what's real and what's not. Your love, light, and soul are real, and they will always be—no matter what.

It's a lifelong lesson to replace fear with hope. You might find that it helps to get to know what *hope* and *fear* mean for you personally. Learning the definitions of the words is simple, but identifying them within yourself is more of an awakening experience.

If you find that you have hope in your heart and fear in your head, then put your focus on your heart.

Speaking of your heart, let's talk about love, baby. Think about the people you love. If every one of these people betrayed you, would you still love any of them? If so, you have unconditional love for them.

Unconditional love is love you have no matter what. That is the kind of love many parents have for their kids.

Conditional love, on the other hand, is based on fear. When you have conditional love, you love them as long as they keep doing what they're doing. If they changed toward you, however, your love might change like it's on a dimmer switch.

You can aspire to achieve unconditional love. It's better that way because it's free of judgments. Unconditional love also detaches you from outcomes and hurt feelings when people act like humans who make mistakes. This is a good thing. Stay true to you and to your divinity.

When it comes to relationships, have you heard that you should put yourself first so that you're whole within yourself? You really shouldn't look for someone else to make you feel whole. Feel how good it feels to feel good within your own self. There's nothing wrong with being single, especially if you're happy. Besides, you'll be better for the person you're eventually going to be with if you're already whole individually.

A Zen approach to dating has you getting out and having fun, being with other people, being true to yourself, and letting go of expectations about the people you're meeting—just be in the moment.

When you're in a relationship, what happens if you stop acting like that person is special? What happens when you have a plant and forget to water it? You don't blame the plant when it dies. But when a relationship ends, most people blame the other person. How about pretending the person is that plant and giving him or her the attention they need just like you would give the plant the water it needs?

There is no right or wrong way to do a relationship, but the Zen approach to relationships has you acknowledging problems and staying open to them so you can begin to understand where they came from. If the problems originated from your life before the relationship, admitting that to yourself can help you save the relationship before it's ruined.

Put yourself in check when you're making assumptions, projecting into the future, or expecting specific things from your mate. Don't attach yourself to what you think a relationship should be like.

Love others and allow them to do what they have to do to get through life. Don't fear.

Think about situations in your own life. How can you apply the Zen way?

Unnecessary fear means you're not putting full trust in the higher powers that love you.

Hope, on the other hand, connects you to heaven like a magical cord. It attaches to you like a light holding you in the darkness. The more you cling to it, the better.

While you're here on earth, your soul is a little vulnerable. Imagine magically wrapping yourself up in a tight blanket of hope, love, and light and not letting it go until you're safely back home in heaven. You'll be so comforted, and you'll know you're in the exact right place.

Have you ever had déjà vu, where it seems like you've been in that same situation, in that same scene, with the same people, and all the other details are exactly the same, but it only lasts a few seconds? That kind of déjà vu is a miracle! It's a signal to your soul that you are on the right track in your chart. You have been in that situation before, because you planned it into your chart before you came to earth and let it stick in your memory as a way to comfort your soul with reassurance that you're on the right track.

The things that you think of as coincidences or synchronicity are often the same sort of signals to your soul that you're on the right track. Good job!

Keep noticing these affirmative signs. A Zen way of life can be your superpower for living in the now and getting the most out of this life. Once you clear your mind of all your fears, you start noticing miracles all around you that you hadn't noticed before. Talk about magic!

Playtime!
Always Share

Share something today. It can be anything of material worth. Make sure it's something that you like, something you don't want to lose, and something the other person would like to keep. Notice how it makes you feel—you'll have it back soon.

-Or-

Write down everything you buy. If you feel like that would be too much work because you shop for groceries and household necessities for your family, just write down everything you buy on impulse. If you follow this plan, you might choose not to buy it just because then you wouldn't have to write it down.

-Or-

Write down what you want to buy without buying it just yet. Each week, look at what you wrote three weeks prior. If you still want it, you can decide to buy it. Chances are, you'll wonder why you even wanted it in the first place.

Zany Zen

Ask a few people, individually, what they want. Notice if you get answers about what they don't want. Do you see how their thoughts could become a destiny that's opposite of what they want, especially since a big portion of the brain doesn't even comprehend the word *not*?

-Or-

Notice each time you're making life more difficult than it has to be. Make it better by being Zen-like and realizing that, even though things perceived as bad need to happen, they don't need to affect you in such a negative way.

-Or-

Practice living in the now. You can call this game *Now and Zen*.

Emotions Shmemotions

Notice any negative emotions you're holding on to and write them down here:

_____

_____

_____

_____

_____

_____

Now, let them go!

Notice any positive emotions you have and write them down here:

_____

_____

_____

_____

_____

_____

Now, memorize them and hold on to them. Come back to them whenever you want to feel the happiness these feelings bring. They're there as gifts for you to use as you choose.

-Or-

As you move through your day, whenever you have an icky feeling, notice it and turn it into a good feeling. If necessary, fake it till you make it. You can smile or even laugh and hold on to the feeling that the smile or laugh gave you. Don't let it go. If it slips away, grab it back. Keep purposefully grabbing it back until it's such a natural habit that you don't even have to think about it anymore.

-Or-

Look back on your life and see it objectively because the emotions aren't tied to it like they were when you were living it. See your present and future hardships in the same way.

Here's to Hoping and Forgetting the Fear

Write down the fears you have right now that you'd like to shake off:

_____

_____

_____

_____

_____

_____

Change each fear to a hope:

_____

_____

_____

_____

_____

_____

Instead of fearing away hope, here's to hoping away fear!

Stars and Psychics

Have you ever heard of star children? Don't they sound mystical? Maybe you are one! We all came to earth with a special purpose. We want to expand our souls and learn about our spirituality in a place where negativity seems to overshadow the love that is right there for us if we search for it.

Since life on earth is so tough, some highly developed souls came here with the special purpose of challenging certain beliefs so they can bring in a new sense of integrity. These evolved spirits are referred to as indigos, and they are star children. A lot of indigo children were born in the 1970s. Many of them were born with determined—or even hot—tempers because being so headstrong would help them with their missions.

Since humans tend to forget their soul charts, many do not realize they are considered indigos, but their souls definitely remember and understand the mission. A lot of indigos can see spiritual energy, and many of them are clairvoyant. Did you already make the connection between the color of their nickname and the color of the third eye chakra? Indigo is the color of the brow chakra, or the third eye, which is the chakra of inner knowing, or intuition. Their vibrations are high, and their intuition is keen. Can you think of ways people with these characteristics could make positive changes in our world?

Indigos see life as a time to create. Since creating means changing, they feel like they should be able to make big life changes anytime they see fit in order to follow their passions—even if their passions change a lot.

It's not easy for these highly evolved spirits to conform to dysfunction, and they're sensitive to dishonesty so they know intuitively when they're being manipulated or patronized.

Because of their differences, a lot of indigo children are mislabeled as having attention deficit disorder or attention deficit with hyperactivity disorder, and the medications for those disorders can cause them to lose their natural gifts! Humans, huh?

Were you born in a later generation but feel like you're spiritually evolved with a highly developed soul? Maybe you're a crystal child! Crystal children have their own special mission. The mission is to follow the indigo children's newly opened paths of integrity in order to teach new lessons of empowerment and love. They're leading the way for humanity with happiness, delight, forgiveness, and even tempers. They might hug people in need seemingly out of the blue.

A lot of crystal children have trouble learning to speak. Children who have trouble learning to speak are often labeled autistic. They are medicated accordingly. This isn't a bad thing, since human adults who label and medicate children with difficulties are just trying to help, but a lot of the medication has unfortunate side effects, including masking the true essence of the individual.

The mission of a crystal child is to help the people of earth develop intuitive and telepathic abilities. They make up ways to communicate—sounds, sign language, songs, and other things they invent. We're learning, through them, to communicate less with words and more with our spiritual vibes! Very cool!

With the help of crystal children, we'll all communicate more easily. We'll become more aware of our intuition and feelings. We'll be able to be more honest and direct with our thoughts because we'll understand them better, and we'll be able to communicate faster and more telepathically. We won't have to rely on the spoken word as much as we do now.

Crystal children are named for their multicolor opalescent auras. They're naturally fascinated with crystals and rocks. Like indigos, they see life as a time of creation and change. They feel like they should be able to reinvent themselves anytime they want to in order to follow their passions whenever their passions change.

Although any type of star child can be born at any time, the biggest wave of indigos was born first so they could lead the way by breaking down anything that lacked integrity. The biggest wave of crystals followed the path to fill that void with compassion.

Following the biggest wave of crystal children is the biggest wave of rainbow children.

Can you guess what color aura rainbow children give off? That's right—the colors of the rainbow! They match our natural chakras. Their bright rainbow auras will help instill a new sense of health and balance within us just by being near them.

Rainbow children are born pretty much at their spiritual peaks, so they don't have the same life lessons as the rest of us. They are here mainly to help us move on the path toward love. Because they're at their spiritual peaks, they're intuitive and tend to be fearless.

Rainbow children might be hyperactive, and many can go without much food or sleep. They smile a lot and recover more easily from emotions than the rest of us do. They're naturally filled with happiness, and they're colorful, creative and confident. They don't hold on to aggression. Instead, they tend to focus on kindness, giving to others, and divinity. They're able to easily bring people together and form bonds. They might be seen as stubborn because it's easy for them to express what they want and need.

Collectively, indigos, crystals and rainbows are referred to as star children. Do you know any star children? Many star children are quite intuitive. Psychics are also intuitive. I'm referring to highly intuitive individuals and not to people who just call themselves psychic.

What is a psychic? How does a person come to know things that others can't see? It all has to do with vibration levels. Spiritual energy has an extremely high vibration level.

Since babies are fresh from the spiritual world, they still have high vibrations and can see spiritual energy. As we grow up, most of us lose this ability as negativity wears us down and brings down our vibration levels.

Some adults, however, keep or develop their high vibrations. They hold on to their spiritual abilities. That's why some people are psychic, and others are so far from being psychic that they don't even believe it's possible.

It doesn't help that some people are making money by pretending to be more psychic than they are. If you want to get real advice from a psychic, do some research to know whether he or she is the real deal. If you're unsure, it's okay to have fun with it—just be sure not to put too much stake into what they say.

Psychic ability can be hereditary, and it can be learned. Learned psychic ability comes from meditation and truly listening to and trusting your intuition.

I had some experiences with psychics at the turning point of my career. At a mini retreat, we had a *message circle* or an *angel circle*. Everyone was encouraged to input her own intuitions about the others. When it was my turn, I wanted to ask what path to take for my career; instead, the woman in charge insisted on telling me what she saw over me.

She said a relative who had recently passed was there to help me and had been coming to me in my dreams. The relative wanted me to trust my intuition and know that she was there to help as I walked through the fire. She explained that everything I was worried about would be okay and to ask her for signs since I couldn't see her.

Sure enough, I had dreamed about my grandma three times in the previous week (she had died about two months earlier). In the dreams, I was sitting next to her on her couch, but she didn't seem to be talking to me. I guess she was, but I just hadn't known.

I fully trusted that my grandma was with me after that, and it opened up a whole new world of connection between her spirit and mine. Before she died, I had asked her what I should do with my life as far as a new career goes, and she was able to guide me after her death in ways that still seem magical years later.

Other women in the circle said they could see a light shining on me, a bud opening up, a pink rose, three oranges (three is a holy number), the song, "That Girl Is on Fire," fearless courage ready to open, an elephant, an urge to be thoughtful of myself for my own emotions, and advice to take care of myself. These symbols are up for interpretation, but I had not discussed my worries or life situation with them at all.

Another reading I had was at a holistic health fair. I hadn't spoken about my worries or my life situation with that woman, either. She said that I'm headstrong and that anything I decide to do, I will do, and that I have the head-heart connection. She said that career-wise I was about to turn a corner and was almost to my goal. She mentioned that I do spend time on meditation, but that I also need to carry the effects of the meditation with me.

She asked if I knew that I was a healer. I told her I had recently been attuned to Reiki, and she said that Reiki would give me the confidence to heal, but that I could do it without the specific Reiki energy. She said that I needed to decide what to do with it. She mentioned that I spent a lot of time trying to figure out how to get clients to come to me, but that I didn't have to worry about that because the people who needed me would come to me. She said I might do social service or spiritual service and that

I should try it all. I could help other people but might feel melancholy and frustrated when things were moving too slowly.

She said I had a nurturing, wise spirit and that the smallest gesture could make others feel like they have all my attention. She said I might spend more time teaching adults who wanted to be there and that I should ask for clear direction when meditating. She told me to open the door and let it in, trust my guidance, and develop a relationship with my guides. She said a change was coming and that I was holding on to something that I needed to let go; I was answering a higher calling. She was pulling tarot cards, and with the last card, she said, "This is why you can let go: your cup overflow-eth."

I would never have thought those types of things about myself without those people pointing them out to me. Everything sounded so mystical and mysterious at the time, but as time went by, I could see the connections more clearly.

We'll see what happens from here, but it's a very interesting experiment either way!

See what results you can get with your experiments. You've already been born, so you can't just become a star child if you're not already one, but the higher your vibrations rise, the more psychic you'll become. All of us have the power—you just need to trust yourself and let it happen as you work to raise your vibrations.

Playtime!
Are You a Star Child?

You might be a star child and not even know it. Trust your intuition.

Jot down the qualities you have that fit star children:

_____

_____

_____

_____

_____

_____

See This

Play with these steps to develop your psychic abilities:

Choose a situation, and guess one thing that will happen soon.

_____

_____

Write down the feelings that make you think it will happen soon.

_____

_____

Wait for it. Did it happen? Write down the results.

_____

_____

Make the connections between your answers.

_____

_____

Repeat. The connections you make with the last step will show you how to work with your intuition. Keep raising your vibes—and you'll get there!

Mysterious Beings

Mysterious spirits and other beings definitely hang out around us. Do you think the creator of the entire universe really just made us low-vibe, physically formed humans? If you only believe in science, do you believe the science of living things can only exist on this earth?

Have you ever been haunted? There are people who have died, and for whatever reason, their spirits didn't make their way to heaven—maybe they don't even know they're dead! If they don't know they're dead, they're confused because they don't know why people can't see them!

Another possibility for why some spirits hang around after the body dies is that they don't want to be dead because they have unfinished business here—maybe it's a job they feel responsibility for finishing, to wait for a lost love, for revenge, or from fear that they won't be accepted into heaven. If that is the case, they probably don't want you around, and they'll try to scare you out.

Imagine being in a room and no one notices you're there. Can you imagine being in your own home where other people are living and carrying on as though you're not there? What would you do to get attention? You'd probably scare them if you had to. These spirits might move things or create breezes. If that doesn't work, they might do something that seems a lot scarier to force us to take action.

Another reason ghosts seem scary is if they have injuries that caused their physical death. If you see a sick, deformed, or emotionally pained being, it is a ghost of a person who has died. It's not a spirit from heaven or a guide (they are not scary).

If you can see ghosts, you're clairvoyant. It's a natural ability for some people. Can you imagine how scary it would be to be clairvoyant and not know it? If this is the case for you, and you want the ghosts to be gone, you can just tell them to leave. Say something like, "Hey, you're dead—go to the light." If you coerce them to the light of their soul's home, they'll be gone from you. There are people who do this as a profession if you want help.

Ask for love and light to protect you. Whether you see spirits or not, visualizing a bright white light protecting you and bouncing negative energy away from you is a good practice.

As far as I know, scientists have yet to prove that ghosts exist, but they also haven't proven that they don't exist. Think of how much science has proven that wasn't believed in before, like the earth being round. The proof of ghosts could be just around the corner.

You don't have to believe it, especially if you can't see them and don't like the possibility of being frightened. It's okay to remain purposefully, mindfully sheltered. As with everything else in the world, pay most attention to what you believe deep in your soul.

So many parts of life are mysteries—so let it be mysterious. Speaking of mysterious, do you believe in aliens? Of course aliens exist!

You might also be keeping yourself purposefully, mindfully sheltered to let yourself believe that the one who created the entire, humongous universe only put living beings on one tiny little earth. The same power that created us and loves us unconditionally created creatures in other places as well, so we don't have to be afraid of aliens. We're only scared of them because we don't know what to expect from them. Oh, yeah, and probably because of all the scary movies perpetuating fears. No worries in reality, though!

One day I was driving on the interstate from Milwaukee toward Chicago, and I saw an airplane hovering in the sky. Airplanes don't hover, do they? It was lower than planes usually go, directly over a neighborhood, and not going anywhere. It was not a helicopter.

I thought it was my imagination, at first, and I kept looking. It never moved. Once home, I went to You Tube and searched for hovering airplanes. Other people had seen them as well. I kept looking for articles and explanations, and I found two main theories: they are government inventions to spy on us or they are alien inventions, also to spy on us.

If it was a government spy plane, it would have been hidden better. These planes were not hidden, and they were so close on a bright and sunny day.

I found a story about an aircraft that was shaped like an airplane and hovered over a man's neighborhood periodically. Whenever he would push the record button on his video camera, it moved away. When he stopped recording, it stopped as well. You can draw your own conclusions, including whether he was even telling the truth, but it sure aligns well with what I've read in spiritual books. I've read that aliens are souls that have incarnated on other planets, and they want to help us because we're on the most self-destructive planet.

Earth is the least heavenly, least peaceful place in the universe. The aliens are more peaceful and less criminal than we are, and we truly don't have anything to fear (except fear itself) when it comes to aliens. As far as I can tell, they are hovering in inventions that were made to look like airplanes so they could remain somewhat undercover while they watch what we do so they can plan the best way to help us learn how to be more peaceful. They want to help our planet because we're the worst off. They refer to our world as the Blue Jewel. That doesn't sound so scary, does it? I don't think we have to worry about them kidnapping us or harming us.

I love it when science and spirituality mix. When you add humor, it's golden! I was watching *The Late Late Show with James Corden,* and the guests were Neil deGrasse Tyson, a well-known scientist, and Andy Samberg, a comedian.

James, the host, told Andy, the comedian, to ask Neil, the scientist, a couple of questions.

Andy asked, "Are we alone in the universe?"

Neil responded, "We might not be considered among the most intelligent out there … You *can't* think we're alone once you study how common our ingredients of life are, in the universe, the atoms of our body, hydrogen, oxygen, carbon—they're the three most common chemically active ingredients in the universe. We're not made of special stuff. And, we're based on carbon, we're carbon-based life, which is an extremely sticky element that makes molecules all across the periodic table, so if there was any kind of biology upon which you would base on an element, it would be carbon, and we are such an example of that life. Not only that—life got started almost as fast as it possibly could have, in the early earth, after earth cooled down from meteor impacts that made us. Once it cooled down, complex molecules formed. Within a hundred million years, life appeared. So, you combine these facts and then you look at the expanse of the fourteen-billion-year age of the universe with a hundred billion stars in our galaxy and a hundred billion galaxies, to *suggest* that we are the only life in the universe would be *inexcusably egocentric*."

Some scientists ask, "Why do some of us assume those from other planets would be so different from us?"

Others ask, "Why do we even call them aliens?"

Some see a lot of limitations to getting in touch with aliens, and say that in order for us to successfully get in touch with and communicate with them, they would have to have the same perception of time as us, speak the same language as us, and be at the same level of development as us. Some scientists say that aliens use scalar waves, and that we will soon receive messages from alien life forms.

Did you know that the United Nations has a spokesperson for the human race? She is an ambassador for earth, otherwise known as the UN ambassador to extraterrestrials. That would be a fun job!

Who knows what's out there? It wasn't that long ago that we didn't even know there were planets outside our own solar system. As always, draw your own conclusions. The conclusion I draw is that aliens have a different frequency, so we aren't able to see them any easier than we can see spirits.

Some people see higher vibrations, some have seen aliens, and some have seen spirits.

For the most part, we aren't meant to have proof yet. Otherwise, we would have it. Mysteries are mysterious on purpose.

Let it be so—life is a mystery to have fun with!

Playtime!
Goofy Ghouls

Think about this:

Does the idea of ghosts scare you? _____

Why? _____

Think back as far as you can to where that fear came from. _____

What have you heard about ghosts? _____

Did this come from another person or various people? _____

Can you realize that those fears originally came from a place of fear? ____

_____

It's not necessary to be afraid!

Aliens Only Wanna Help and That's No Joke

Answer these questions:

Can you think of a reason there would be life on this one planet and not on any other?

_____

_____

_____

_____

_____

What do you think other planets would be like with people who were different from us but the same as each other?

_____

_____

_____

_____

_____

-Or-

Write a story answering these questions:

What do you think aliens look like?
What do you think they sound like?

How would they communicate with each other?
How do they work?
How do they play?
Can they see us?
What do they want with us?
Why would they want to help us?
How would they help us?

_____

_____

_____

_____

_____

_____

_____

_____

_____

_____

_____

_____

_____

Connect Four

Let's explore how your chart, free will, the law of attraction, and the ideas of karma tie together.

Have you ever tried to push through a door that was locked? Have you ever tried to push through a door that didn't open because you were pushing in the wrong direction? Or, worse, have you pushed on a door that opened into the wrong bathroom? I've been there and done that more often than I'd like to admit!

What do you do when the door is locked? Do you break the lock and cry when you see that no one wants you there? Do you walk away gracefully, being okay with not getting into the room?

Think about how nice it is when a door opens easily for you. Maybe someone opens the door for you, and there's even a welcoming committee serving potato chips on the other side.

It's the same in life with metaphorical doors. Have you ever wanted something that you didn't get? Ha! Of course! We all have. That's life. How about when you got something you didn't even want and it made life better? Surely, you can think of something!

Some doors are open for you, and some aren't. That's just the way life is, and the more you're okay with that, the better.

Think about how much of the stress in your life came from wanting something and trying to control life so that you could get what you want. If you really think about it, you'd probably realize most of your stress has come from trying to control things to make them the way you think they should be. Everyone talks about setting goals and planning for the future. Somehow, that leads us to believe we should assume control over every little thing. When we realize everything's out of our control, it just adds more stress!

Instead of holding on to that stress, it would be easier to just trust that things that are meant for you will come, and things that aren't meant for you won't come. Deal with it—it's easier that way. If something you thought was perfect for you slipped through your fingers, it just wasn't your thing. Be patient for what is in store for you when the time is right. Maybe a similar door will open to you in the future, and maybe it won't.

You could make a promise to yourself right now. The new plan is to go through the doors that are open for you and not to force more. You just have to be on the lookout for opportunities that come your way. What a load off!

Now let's talk about doors to get you the heck out of toxic environments that bring you down. There are many ways to handle these situations. First, try to be the light for others by bringing higher vibrations to the people and to the place. Keep trying!

If it doesn't work, figure out if it's because this door is closing to you altogether. Maybe you're supposed to leave. If you feel like a door is closing on you, get out before it slams shut painfully. You need courage to leave certain situations, but that's okay. Muster up the courage and just do it.

You deserve to be happy. If you aren't getting some inner happiness out of your life or job, you can consider that a sign that you're off your path. You were never meant to stay miserable. If you're miserable and off track, there are ways to find happiness and other ways to pay the bills—lots and lots of ways. If you let your frustrations keep you down, you can make yourself physically sick. Don't let your miserable feelings get you down any more than necessary to give you a shove in the right direction. Don't resist your life's path.

There's no point in trying to swim upstream. Let go of trying to control life and float blissfully downstream to where your successes wait patiently for you. Flowing downstream doesn't mean doing nothing. Be active in your plans—assert what you want and why you want it—and then let go of the need to control the details of what actually happens.

What about the people in your life who make you miserable? There are a lot of different reasons people affect you that way. You have to listen to your intuition to figure out the reason.

If there weren't people in your life to make you a little nuts, how would you learn certain lessons? You might have a lesson to learn in patience, acceptance, letting go, or standing strong within yourself. It might be a test for you to figure out what matters and what doesn't matter. Maybe you're meant to learn how to get away from the person altogether—and stay away.

Learn your lesson, whatever it may be, and then be done with it. If you have it in you, try to feel gratitude for the person for helping you learn your lessons. It can be easier said than done, but you owe it to yourself to give it a shot.

Part of being human is feeling disconnected, at least some of the time, from your purpose, whether it's the purpose of your life as a whole or the hour in front of you. When you feel lost, you might chase after jobs or relationships that aren't meant for you. Instead, find what's right for you for the direction of your day and for your future within the truth of your own soul.

While you're searching, remember to flow with your own tide. Society can be—and often is—wrong. Albert Einstein flowed with the tide he chose. If he had flowed with the tide of society, he wouldn't have had all the success he had. This is true for a lot of the people in the past, present, and future—and most likely for you!

Here's one experiment for recognizing doors that are meant for you:

When you have a decision to make, pretend wholeheartedly that you made the decision one way and concentrate on how it makes you feel in your stomach, body, mind and heart. Concentrate on how your life would be affected. Wait and sit in that feeling until you are positive about the feeling you're getting. Then pretend wholeheartedly that you made the opposite decision. Whichever choice felt better, or less bad, is the one to pick. It will be the one that feels right in the end.

Here are some questions to help you contemplate which doors are meant for you. Don't just think about the answers—try to actually feel them.

- Do I see myself through the eyes of others, my brain, or my soul?
- What do I love to do and wish I had more time for?
- What are the qualities of people who inspire me?
- What are my good qualities?

Here is some advice for going through doors that are meant for you:

- Forget about what other people think.
- Forget about what you think you "should" do.

- Be quiet with yourself with your eyes closed.
- See yourself through the eyes of your own soul.

It might also help to talk your choices out—to earthly beings or those on a higher realm. Do you really want help knowing which doors are open for you and which are locked with the key thrown away? Can you admit to yourself that you're worth more spiritual love and guidance than you could ever hope for? Because you are!

Do you want clear signs? Okay, then—you got it! Ask for signs, and be specific.

When you're asking for signs, you'd like to know when you're being given an answer, right? Our questions are always answered, but we don't always know it because we can't hear them. They don't usually come with actual words.

It's important to understand this when you're on the lookout for signs. If it comes with a good feeling, it's probably a sign. If it comes with a negative feeling, it's likely paranoia. Let those negative feelings go, because paranoia is not a sign from your guides; it's a human quality.

You can ask for a concrete sign. Make sure it's something that means something to you, so you're more likely to spot it when it appears. You can ask to find a nickel if an answer is *yes* and a penny if it's *no*. Don't worry if it takes time. Just be sure to remember what you asked and what the answers will signify. You can also ask for something along the lines of seeing a certain word or color within the next hour.

As for feelings, you could ask for the right decision to give you a feeling of happiness or excitement, and the wrong decision to give you a feeling of apprehension. Be on the lookout for signs even when you're not specifically asking for them.

When I drop something or put my pants on backward, I usually take it as a sign to slow down. If I don't slow down, I usually drop something else or put my pants on backward again! I try to listen better and take the day step by step in the moment, being in the here and now.

Do you know who gives you the signs you're asking for? Your spirit guides! They're always around you, waiting for you to ask them for help. Sometimes I'll ask my spirit guide to tickle my nose for proof he's there.

That might sound crazy, but I'm asking for a sign, and I can always feel it! Sometimes I have to wait for it, but it comes. Sometimes I have to actually ask him to stop because it won't stop itching. That's a very awesome and comforting way to be annoyed!

While you're working on communicating for signs that will lead you through the proper doors, here are some facts about your chart:

- You designed your life path before you got to this great school of earth.
- Your spirit was in the safety of heaven when you drew up this plan. You probably planned for worse than you wish you would have.
- You planned an emotion to work on.
- You had optional life paths to choose from.
- You had options for which areas of life would be the most difficult.
- You left one area of your life open; you didn't clearly define it in your chart.

Please respect yourself and others—no matter what life path the person is on. Some might be ugly, but that's just the way we learn and grow. Many people who believe in reincarnation believe we come here enough times to experience each life path so we can learn as much as possible. If this is true, you really and truly have no reason to ever judge any life path! We've all been there or will be there—on purpose and for good reason.

Life themes mean different things for different people. One soul who chooses poverty learns by dealing with it, and another person learns by overcoming it.

Life themes include rescuer, warrior, wealth, poverty, survival, healer, justice, lawfulness, leader, experiencer, activator, aesthetic (like music or drama), peacemaker, builder, catalyst, cause-fighter, humanitarian, victim, victimizer, controller, performer, manipulator, spirituality, patience, banner-carrier, winner, psychic, responsibility, intellectual, temperance, tolerance, harmony, emotionality, fallibility, infallibility, analyzer, persecutor, persecution, follower, loner, loser, irritant, passivity, rejection and pawn.

After thinking about these, write which ones resonate with your life:

_____

_____

_____

Options for the part of life that would be the most difficult include:

- social life
- career
- health
- family
- finances
- love
- spirituality

Which did you choose?

_____

_____

Don't be afraid of starting these conversations with other people! Soul-searching will come easier if we can talk about it with others. Also, don't let having a chart fool you into thinking you don't have free will! How do you think free will and the law of attraction tie in to your chart?

You definitely have free will to ask the law of attraction to work for you. The law of attraction says that whatever you think about most will manifest in your life. If you think of yourself as rich, you'll be rich. If you think of yourself as broke, you'll be broke. If you think your life is great, your life will be great. If you think it's difficult, it'll be difficult.

When you're trying to work your magic wand with the law of attraction, it's not about wishing you had something. If you think, *I wish I had that,* you will get it—in that you'll get wishing you had it.

Instead, think about having it now. Don't be attached to outcomes. How do you focus solely on what you want to attract without being attached to the outcome? Sometimes attempting to make the law of attraction work feels like trying to control life. How do you rely on the law of attraction manifesting what you want while letting go of control?

You have to align your feelings so you're on the same vibrational level as what you wish for. It won't manifest if your feelings are telling you that you don't deserve it.

Let's use money as an example. Humans made money, and it's a form of energy. You deserve to have enough money, and it's okay to intend to be financially abundant. If somewhere deep down, you believe you don't deserve abundance, it won't come to you. If you think you deserve it, but you don't believe you already have enough, it might not work for you. If you realize that you already have enough, and maybe even loosen your purse strings, you'll match the vibrational level of having enough and you will be abundant.

Give it a shot by changing your belief system. Experiment by leaving bigger tips or giving more to charity and see what happens. You'll realize there is enough abundance in the world for you since you're a very important part of this universe.

No matter what, remain hopeful and focus on the positive aspects of what you hope for when you do think about it (rather than focusing on your lack of it). Be unattached to the actual outcome as you simply live in the now.

I have always believed that a good attitude makes for a much happier life, but I also worry a lot. When I first read that the law of attraction works like magic, I worried that the things I was worried about would happen because I kept worrying. I didn't know how to stop worrying. I looked to a Sylvia Browne book for her opinion. She said not to be paranoid that you'll actually create your fears because fears have nothing to do with programming. Negative thoughts can't alter your chart, but they can delay it. Positive thoughts can make everything speed up, and positivity is the path for gaining higher spirituality. This should give you some comfort if you're a worrier.

Optimism changes your actions, and actions change happenstances. Sometimes things we perceive as bad happen anyway, but that's just the way life is. Learning is a process, and because you don't know what the curriculum is, there are even more steps to the process.

Scientifically, the law of attraction works through positive expectations, cause and effect, and self-fulfilling prophecies. You must work to reprogram your subconscious mind with a new belief system.

If you don't think this pertains to you personally, think about the collective attitude. Society's use of negativity may have caused individual negativity, but each individual can and should rise above it and let the good take over. If everybody in the world thought positively, the world would be a better place. People's negative thoughts make the world so bad in so many ways. People's good thoughts make the world so good in so many ways.

Replace your fears with love, your worries with hope, and negativity with positivity. Watch how the energies of attraction work for you! If it comes down to it, and you don't get what you want because of your chart, you're always welcome to ask that your desires be changed. Not getting what you want won't be so bad if you quit wanting it!

Your chart is like an outline, but you have free will to react however you choose to the things that happen. Your chart will make sure you experience your lessons. Free will leaves it up to you to decide how you experience your lessons.

How will you handle the situations that come into your life? Will you fear them and their results?

Will you take your stresses out on other people, bringing down the energy of everyone around you?

When life seems to beat you over the head, will you still be kind to others?

Will you love through your troubles?

Will you learn from your situations so much that you're excited to help others who go through similar situations?

Will you use the law of attraction, thinking positively no matter what happens because of your chart? There are a lot of decisions you can make about each life situation.

How can you tell which life situations are because of your chart and which you've attracted to yourself? Let's say you had a friend who died after a tragic accident on her way home from your house as a young adult. Neither of you attracted that to make it happen. It was in his or her chart to die, and it was in your chart to be friends during that time, partially so that you would experience the unexpected death of a loved one. It's possible you were meant to experience that because it would lead to soul-searching, probably for the meaning of life. This search for truth deepens your spirituality and raises your vibes, even though the process of the death felt so crushing. I know this is true because I lived through it.

Years later, I quit being a public school teacher and became a yoga instructor and Reiki Master. It was in my chart to switch careers, but the timing had to do with listening to my intuition. My intuition told me I had to leave, but there was also free will at play. If free will had kept me at school longer—if I had chosen to believe it was the only way I could pay the bills and keep my house—the situation would have just gotten worse until eventually I left. Who knows how my dangerously high blood pressure would have affected me by then? I had to experience the lesson until I finally learned it. I had to believe that the one who gave me a soul to expand works in mysterious ways—but also listens and answers even when the answer isn't the one I want. I'd wanted the job that I already had to keep me happy!

Each day, I would daydream of running away from school, running to Hawaii, and doing yoga on the beach. Was it a daydream—or was it my intuition guiding me? The energy of attraction stepped in. Within months, I was earning my yoga certification in Hawaii. Thankfully, I hadn't spent my miserable school time visualizing myself as being jobless and homeless. I'd much rather be attracting myself to Hawaii!

There aren't any specific rules for knowing where your life situations have come from, but you can use your intuition to try to figure it out if you'd like. Meditate on it!

Karma also ties in to our lives. Many of us have an idea of what it means to the general population, but if you research, you'll find that scientists and spiritual teachers have various meanings.

Here are some interpretations:

- If you're nice, others will be nice to you.
- Karma is a backlash for doing wrong.
- Karma is *not* a backlash for doing wrong.

- Karma is your life path. You experience lots of lives to go through all types of life paths. That's how your soul learns everything it sets out to learn.
- You cannot change it.
- You can change it by letting good things into your life.

It's okay that it means different things to different people—that's part of the mystery and fun of life. What does it mean to you? You can keep changing your mind as you keep thinking about it.

Whatever happens in life, exterior conditions cannot create interior conditions unless you let them. You can keep yourself shielded in your soul by asking the divine to shield you. You might settle for trusting the one who should be trusted to do what's right for you as you keep up hope and ask that you be shielded from negativity. Ask for protection from your fears and that they be sent up to be spiritually vanished even as they recur.

Let the fact that you have a chart be comforting to you, appreciate your right to experiment with the law of attraction, and use your free will to be happy anytime and anywhere you want.

Playtime!
Ding-Dong or No Ding-Dong?

What doors have closed on you?

_____

_____

_____

What doors have you tried to go through that weren't open?

_____

_____

_____

What doors were open for you?

_____

_____

_____

What doors do you hope will open for you?

_____

_____

_____

How do you hope to handle it if these doors don't open for you?

_____

_____

_____

-Or-

Meditate using a slow walking meditation toward a doorway to help you intuit what is behind the door that is meant for you. You will know what path to take in whatever situation you find yourself.

Signs, Signs, Everywhere Are Signs

Ask a yes-or-no question and put it out there in the universe. Say what you want the sign to be for a yes answer and what you want the sign to be for a no answer. For example, if you see a billboard or sign with the color red on it, the answer is *yes*, and if you see a billboard or sign with the color blue on it, the answer is *no*.

Party on Your Life Path

Write what you think your life path might be. You might have more than one. Also write how you feel about those life paths.

_____

_____

_____

Do you wish your life path could be different than it is? Why?

_____

_____

_____

What is your most difficult part of life? Do you wish you had chosen a different option?

_____

_____

_____

Attract *This*

Notice your negative thoughts and turn them into positive ones. For example, if you think someone doesn't like you, change it into a positive thought. "She will like me when she knows me better."

Do this with every negative thought you catch yourself having. You'll thank yourself if you do!

Fun Figuring Where It Came From

Think about a part of your life and consider which of the following it came from:

- your chart
- free will
- the law of attraction
- karma

Do You Vibe with Religion? Shamans?

Do you vibe with religion? It's cool if you do, but you don't have to!

What is religion? What is church?

The word *religion* can be defined as a set of beliefs to which you conform. Do you think it's necessary to follow a set of beliefs as defined by other humans? Do you think it's necessary to conform to your own set of beliefs?

Why conform at all? Why not keep exploring and learning? Maybe your beliefs aren't set. Maybe you're keeping your eyes open to learn along the way and don't necessarily agree with anyone else's set beliefs. That's okay!

Church, as opposed to religion, can be defined as a place to worship. Maybe your church is within yourself. That's okay!

If you've ever ventured into a church, you might have felt that many teachings were meant to change how people think and feel. Some teachings resonate with how you feel in your heart and soul, and some teachings don't feel right.

Delving deeply into one religion can lead to restrictions in your beliefs, but there's truly no need to agree with everything a church teaches in order to feel like you have a connection with higher powers, whether inside of that place or anywhere else.

The intention to base life on the divine is the beautiful purpose. Religion was really meant to help people find support for furthering their spirituality with people who think like them. Life shouldn't be done alone—we should do it together. We are supposed to help each other. Helping each other adds to our own energy.

The supreme being is happy we have religions for personal guidance but doesn't want us to haphazardly agree with anyone else's human-made opinions or rules just because we feel we have to. If an idea or suggestion feels good and right to you, go with it. If it doesn't, let it go. Exploring different beliefs, whether you agree with them or not, serves as steps in your learning process.

If our physical world weren't so loud with opinions and unnecessary rules, we would know more clearly what the spiritual truth is.

No religion is worth anything if it doesn't teach love or lead with love. Love is the most important part of divinity. We should accept each other for each other's beliefs. We are not meant to be judgmental of each other in any way.

Books were written, translated, and modified by humans, so we should really be careful about taking everything literally. There's the Bible, the Bhagavad Gita, the Qur'an, the Upanishads, the Talmud, the Book of Mormon, the Vedas, and all the books you can find at bookstores and libraries. These wonderful books all have important ideas to share. Exploring them all and then listening to your own soul about the truth would be the best bet. You have to decide on your own what to take to heart and what to let go.

The Catholic Church gave me the belief in God and the confidence that we're loved unconditionally. That, to me, is worth everything. It also taught me to love others for who they are, forgive others and myself, make morally right decisions, trust in the divine's will more than mine or anyone else's, and much, much more.

But I also developed an unearned feeling of guilt. It wasn't until I was an adult that I realized it, and it took someone else to point it out to me. We were at work, and our boss was behaving like her normal self.

Later, I brought it up to my coworker and said, "I didn't do anything wrong. Why do I feel so guilty?"

She answered, "Are you Catholic?"

I said, "Yes."

She simply said, "That's why."

I sure did feel a sense of relief. I'm not trying to bash the church. I'm trying to help you see how the real truth is within your own soul more than in any given religion. I knew I had no real reason to feel guilty.

What is a Christian? I always thought it was any person who believes in Christ, but I know now that other people think of it totally differently. There's a lot of negativity toward the word, but since it's a very general term, we need to be careful not to judge those who call themselves Christian. You don't even know what they mean by it, since there isn't even a specific solid definition of the word in the Bible.

Bible-based churches lead from the Bible and following Jesus. When Jesus told parables, he was using stories to make points and teach lessons. Stories are meant to teach lessons rather than to necessarily convey literal happenstances. Much of the Bible is made up of stories from different people's points of view. Since stories are often open to interpretation, you have a lot to contemplate when exploring Bible teachings.

Jehovah's Witnesses interpret the Bible more literally and base their beliefs on that literal interpretation. They believe there is a kind and merciful god and that everyone is welcome to have a relationship with him. They also believe that human existence on earth will end soon and that all non-believers will, well ... let's just say they'll wish they had believed. At least some Jehovah's Witnesses believe that their religion is the only true religion and that all other religions are under Satan's control.

The Buddha was a regular person; he was not a supernatural being. His name was Siddhartha Gautama, and his dad kept him sheltered from all negativity. Doesn't that sound great? Well, if you really think about it, doesn't that sound reclusive and boring? One day, Siddhartha busted out and learned all sorts of bad things about the world all at once! Naturally, this left him with a lot of questions about the world, which led him on his quest for deep understanding. When he taught what he learned to others, he became known as the Awakened One. His teachings include that our serenity doesn't depend on situations, but on our reactions to them, and that everyone is capable of the Buddha nature. They also include purifying your heart while cultivating goodness as well as questioning things you hear before you believe them.

The Four Noble Truths explain why suffering exists and how to do away with it. The Four Noble Truths involve the Noble Eightfold Path of Right Understanding, Right Thought, Right Speech, Right Actions, Right Livelihood, Right Effort, Right Mindfulness, and Right Concentration. The Buddha didn't teach about a god creating the universe, but that all things are interconnected and that we continue to create suffering through Karma. Buddhism teaches that we go through reincarnations to experience all situations on life on earth at least once, and that's how we will overcome all different types of negativity.

Hinduism teaches that there's one supreme God and that all divine paths are parts of his light and should be accepted. These divine paths consist of reincarnation to settle our Karma, which is the effect that people cause with their thoughts and actions. They say the universe also undergoes endless cycles of creation, preservation and dissolution.

Tibetan monks and nuns give gratitude for the suffering they go through. They even ask that they have enough suffering to become as wise and compassionate as possible. Now, that's courageous!

There are more than four thousand religions to look into if you're interested. Most religions believe in an afterlife, and every major religion teaches the existence of the soul.

No matter how you honor the divine power, go with what resonates with you. Let the rest go without worrying that you're not quite sure of the whole truth and place no judgment toward others. Even the highest divine being loves us all for who we are, so who are we to judge?

In general, churches are becoming more relaxed than they were in the past, and the people are more accepting, even though theological rules are still in place. Don't hesitate to venture into a new church and try it out. You'll probably be accepted and welcomed, especially since churches as a whole are seeing their numbers drop, and they like to have people walking through their doors!

No matter where you are on Sunday mornings, let your true church be within yourself and let your true religion be within your soul. If you're looking to explore your spirituality without being given a set of rules, you might seek out shamanism. Shamans work without organizations, dogmas or leaders. They say you don't have to believe what they teach, but they hope we're all willing to try it out.

Shamans teach that to change the world, we have to start with ourselves because our thoughts, fears, beliefs and attitudes make their way into the subconscious and turn into reality. The advice is to not take yourself too seriously and to simply smile because it makes you feel better by transmitting harmonizing love energy; this love energy is what brought everything into existence in the first place. When setting intentions, it's important to work from a place of love and the unconditional sharing of the experience of life.

Shamans use pendulums to communicate between the conscious and subconscious minds. The work is in awakening spiritual wisdom, healing, and growing into conscious awareness. They say that since the higher self doesn't have physical ears, worded prayers often go unanswered because they remain unheard. Using words is a good way to clarify your intention in your brain, but to have the prayers answered they should be visualized.

If you're in the habit of using words during prayer and don't feel comfortable breaking that habit, consider keeping your word prayers while adding visualizations to them. It can't hurt! It's a great time to use your imagination to raise your vibrations and access your higher self.

Any connection to the divine is wonderful, and you're encouraged to find the way to connect that works best for you. Don't be afraid to venture into new territory. It might be just what your soul's been striving for.

Playtime!
Whimsical Worship

If you were asked to make up a religion, what would it be like?

What would be taught? _____

What would the services be like? _____

What would you call the divine charge? _____

How would you teach communication with the divine? _____

What would people wear to service? _____

There is a Bible-based church whose dress code is as follows: "Please wear something." Now, that lets you know your favorite football gear is acceptable on a Sunday morning!

No-Shame Shamanism

Research shamanism paying particular attention to how it relates to scientific findings.

-Or-

Research shamanism paying particular attention to how it relates to what you feel in your heart and soul.

The Divine Charge and Gurus

What do you call the higher power? Some options include God, Azna, Allah, Yahweh, the Lord, Jesus, the Higher Power, the Almighty, the Most High, Holy Spirit, the Supreme Being, Creator, the Great I Am, Father, the Universe and Mother Nature. The list could go on and on.

Big Daddy or even Lil Shorty would be fine—as long as you're connecting!

If you find yourself uncomfortable with these, or you don't believe in any deity, you can send your prayers, intentions, or whatever you'd like to call them to your own higher self. After all, we are all one with the universe and the divine.

The human inventions of separate religions have caused a lot of people to become uncomfortable with many of the specific names. A lot of people have been taught to fear being cruelly judged.

"Fear God" is a common phrase when it comes to some religions, but the message often gets crossed because the literal meaning as we know it today means something along the lines of being scared of what will happen to you. The truer meaning is actually for us to have faith that there's a spiritual purpose. It does not, in any way, mean you're going to be punished! Breathe and relax because you don't have to be afraid—not even a tiny bit. You are cherished for being here on earth just to learn about your inner truth. The divine knows it's difficult and is here to help. We just need to figure out how to receive help.

No Matter What You Call the Higher Power:

- Whatever you lack is a blessing in that it's another chance to ask for help. When you desire to have zero problems, you're pretty much just setting yourself up with an unrealistic goal. See problems as opportunities to draw close to the divine who loves you.
- The highest power in our true home of heaven is real. The divine being loves you unconditionally. Did you hear that? I said *you*. And, I said *unconditionally*.

- You are part of it. We all are. Don't insult yourself or bring yourself down. Even if and when you're feeling sick and tired of your own self, you can imagine yourself as divine light. Yes, you are part of the divine!

- Strive to please the divine within yourself rather than the humanness in other people.

- Trust in the timing of the higher powers. There's no need to rush. Keep your mind free of the clutter of your to-do list, knowing that you will get to it in time.

- It's good to realize the higher power knows you better than you know yourself, loves you more than you've ever even dreamed of being loved, and is love. This love is brighter than the brightest sunshine. Think of the clouds when they're covering the sun and blocking it from view. Have you ever been in an airplane on a cloudy day? You fly into the clouds, and then over the clouds, and suddenly the sunshine is so very bright. The sunshine is right there over the clouds even when you can't see it on earth, just like the love from the divine is surrounding you even when you can't see or feel it.

- You can bring your complaints to the divine powers. Talking it out helps, and you can talk to the one in charge and let those problems dissolve into the light right then and there.

- If you let the higher power control your thoughts, you'll have magical thoughts!

- The seemingly separate divine powers are all one, and we are all one with them—even though it doesn't often feel like it. Since we're on earth now and they're not, they're here in spirit. Because they're in higher vibrations and we're in lower vibrations, they can see and hear us, but we can't often see or hear them. That doesn't make it any less real that they are here. We can reach out to them with our hearts and souls.

- If you fail at everything, you still don't deserve punishment because it's unconditional love.

Have you ever wondered, *If God loves me so much, why did he let this happen? How can a god who loves me let me feel this way?*

It's the same reason parents let kids make mistakes. What are college kids doing when their parents aren't around? They might party hard, skip classes, get low grades, and have to learn their own lessons.

You came here as part of this experiment because you wanted to learn how to handle negativity for your own soul. This earth is as far away as we'll ever get from the spiritual world, and that is a fact, but we're also not as far away as we feel.

Jesus was born on earth to be a human with us so we could learn more from him on our vibrational level. Historians have found facts that Jesus really and truly lived on earth. It isn't just a made-up story. His spirit still surrounds us. Let Jesus's spirit be your best friend. He's loving and readily available to help. At such a high vibrational level, his spirit can be in many places at one time.

You can ask for all sorts of things:

- to stick by your side (even though you don't have to ask because his spirit is always there—maybe you let realizing that remind you to say thank you).
- to hug, hold and comfort you. If you choose to be still and feel it, it will become more real to you. This is a very comforting way to fall asleep.
- to shine spiritual energy onto and into any unhealthy or blocked energies and make you whole again.
- to hold out his hands and stream thoughts to you.
- to put words into your head so you can speak them when you're afraid you don't have the words in you.
- to tickle your nose to prove you're not alone.
- to shine over your family, friends, home and pets.

There are lots and lots of spiritual beings you can call on anytime, from anywhere, to help you or guide you in any aspect of life—big or small.

Here are some examples of the ones I'm familiar with:

- personal spirit guides
- spirit helpers

- spirit friends
- Ganesh
- Buddha
- Azna
- the Holy Spirit
- angels
- archangels
- soul mates
- loved ones from earth who've died
- the spirits of humans on earth

To communicate, you can just tune into your soul and quietly say and visualize what you want. Talk like you're talking to a friend. Expect to hear them talking to you in the way that you speak. They don't use words like those in the Bible. They want to communicate with you in the best way they can, and they're happy to make it comfortable for you.

Your personal spirit guides are there for you from the moment you're born and throughout your life. They are spirit friends, and before you were born into this life, you and your spirit guide planned to come here together. They know your chart inside and out, and they help you whether you know they're there or not. If you do know they're there, you can ask for specific kinds of guidance.

Many people who can see clairvoyantly can see spirit guides.

When I taught second grade, a student told me all about her imaginary friend. She said her name was Lily and that Lily always played with her. I asked where Lily was at the moment, and she pointed to her right side. "She's always right here unless we're playing," she said.

That made me smile. Sylvia Browne wrote that very young children can see their spirit guides and that spirit guides stay to your right side unless they decide to move elsewhere for the time being. She said adults usually tell kids it's just an imaginary friend and tell them to stop talking to them. Once they do, their little earth eyes lose sight of them—and they lose their naturally strong connection.

I asked about Lily, and then I asked if her friend could tell her if I had a friend. She said she'd ask and came back to say that I did.

I asked for her name.

She left, returned, and said, "Jason."

I said, "It's a boy?"

She nodded.

I asked, "Is he cute?"

She contorted her face, exclaimed, "Ew!" and walked back to her seat.

Spirit guides give us a special kind of help because they have been humans on earth before, and they know what it's like to be here.

Besides spirit guides, other spirit helpers and spirit friends are there to help you.

Ganesh is the part of the divine that removes obstacles. He's the elephant-headed Hindu deity who's also called Ganesha or Ganapati.

Buddha's spirit is of happiness, positivity and peace. He encourages us to approach situations with love, happiness and peace so that our situations don't become big problems. He teaches that problems only arise if we respond to difficulties with negativity.

Azna is the mother god. Azna and the father god have been in this together since the very beginning, but the mother god was left out of the early teachings. She's a loving mother who is easy to connect with emotionally. She's also an awesome healer. She carries a sword and cuts through our pain so we can be healed.

The Holy Spirit is said to be the love between the father and mother god. You are a part of that!

It's good to know that angels and archangels are plentiful. They're all around us and can help with different situations.

Here are examples from just a small fraction of the angels available to you:

- Archangel Raziel is the angel of mysteries and helps you find trust in divine timing. He knows your chart and works with abundance and free will. It's said that he holds the secrets of the universe.
- Archangel Raphael helps heal you from your emotions, including heartache and addictions.
- Archangel Michael can cut energy cords that are holding you back and clear your whole body of them by vacuuming out your negative energies and balancing your moods. He's also the angel

of protection and peace. He can help you become more abundant, including with money, since it's energy—just like anything else.

- Archangel Metatron balances your chakras.
- Gabriel brings you hope and strength.
- Uriel brings new beginnings by blessing you with creativity. Ask for help in turning your disappointments into blessings and in trusting, letting go of the past, moving forward and forgiving.
- Archangel Jopuel helps you see your life through the eyes of the divine. How divinely beautiful does that sound?
- Angel Gamliel can get you a great parking space.
- Archangel Sandalphon helps you use your talents and stay focused on what you're meant to do with your life.
- Archangel Jophiel gives courage for your specific life lessons.
- Archangel Peliel helps you trust your intuition.
- Aktriel is the angel of the crown chakra.

Ask angels for help with lost objects, appliances and computers. Angels communicate without using words, so don't worry that you don't hear them responding to you.

Once, I asked Aktriel to open my crown as I was falling asleep. Soon, I felt a force sweeping over my head, down to my feet, and back up through my head again. I got chills all down my legs. I remembered reading about the movement going from head to toes and back to the head. The next day, I had to keep reminding myself of the feeling because I was afraid I'd forget it easily like a dream. I prayed that my crown would stay open and that I'd be able to learn anything I needed more easily because of it.

Angels have saved me at least twice in my life. When I had finished painting my bedroom and was tearing the paint tape down from the ceiling, I stood on the dresser thinking I could just give it one more tug instead of getting the ladder. Well, I was right. I couldn't do it without falling off the dresser, though! I fell from the top of the dresser and landed on my back between the dresser and the wall. The TV cords were plugged in, and an open bottle of water landed on top of me. My phone was in the other room, I was alone, and the house doors were locked.

What a mess I could have been in—and what pain I could have been in! Instead, it felt like I had landed on a cloud. I didn't get so much as a bruise. I wasn't even scared! Do you think this was luck? Angels?

Another time, I had chosen a different way to get to work than usual. I was driving down a highway at the highest speed allowed and didn't see that I was approaching a stop sign at an intersection. A huge truck was already stopped at his stop sign, which meant that he was about to head into the intersection thinking I was going to stop. I didn't.

This time, I *was* scared. I turned the steering wheel, hoping to at least reduce the impact, and the *very* next thing I knew, I was safely on the intersecting road—ahead of the truck and driving perfectly within the center of the lane at the correct speed. It seemed to have happened in a split second.

Do you think it was luck? Mad driving skills? I felt as though a big group of angels had come to my rescue, carried my car over the gutter, and placed it in the safest place it could be.

I know there are a lot of theories as to what really could have been happening, but I don't even care because—no matter what—something saved me, and it wasn't myself. Whatever it was, I'm thankful.

We don't have to speak to any of our spirit friends with words. You could try speaking to them via your imagination, visualization, heart or soul. When we connect with our souls, we connect with our spirit friends as well.

It's likely that your one true soul mate didn't come to earth at the same time as you. This way, he or she is more readily available to help you spiritually no matter where you are. You can call on that mate for companionship anytime.

You also have a lot of other friends on the other side. One night, as I was falling asleep, I asked for friends just to hang out and have fun with me. I don't remember the dream I had, but I remember it being a ton of fun. I had to laugh to myself when I woke up. I felt like I was just getting home from the best time out with the best friends I'd ever had!

You can talk to loved ones from earth who've died. Their spirits can hear you and be next to you. It may take them some time to learn how to communicate with you, but keep at it because it will be amazing.

A friend of mine died after a car accident, and I missed her very much. One night before bed, I told the main guy in heaven that I wanted to laugh with her again. That night, I dreamed that she was sitting at the foot of my bed. We were laughing so hard together. It lasted a long time, and then I slept great. I woke up feeling like I had closure. I felt so at peace that she was happy. I got up, and my stomach was as sore as it would be the day after a bunch of sit-ups. I realized I had been laughing in my bed, which made me realize that my visit with my friend was more than just a dream. Pretty cool, huh?

So, who else can you call on? Well, don't be afraid to talk to people here on earth. Love each other! We weren't meant to go through life alone. We've got each other for a reason. We can't do it alone, and we shouldn't bother trying. Have you ever heard that it "takes a village"? That's not just about raising kids—unless you think of all of us as kids. Doesn't that sound like more fun, anyway?

Try not to let your plans interfere with the people purposefully put in your path. If someone wants to talk to you when you're busy with your own plans, think of another saying: We plan, and God laughs. Those people are in your path for a reason.

We're meant to connect with each other, love one another as we love ourselves, and love ourselves more than we already do. We're all broken in different ways. Find someone to open up to about your problems. Talking to another person can help you see things more clearly. Our brokenness can come with a lot of shame, but if you open up to others, you might get over your embarrassment and shame, connect on a surprisingly deep level, and begin to heal more than ever.

You can try talking to someone you already know or join a group. There are counselors and community groups out there—you just have to find one that works for you. An acquaintance might be more than you expect and could even turn into a close friend.

Listen to others. No one wants to be around someone who whines all the time, but if you let people vent to you, they'll soon feel better, be happier and be more fun to be around. Set an intention not to absorb their bad energy. You'll raise their vibrations by listening so they feel lighter, and you'll feel lighter in the process. You both become more centered and kind. Higher vibrations all around!

Even when you're being a good listener, don't believe rumors. Listening to rumors perpetuates them. Stories change from one person to another. Even if the story is true, you're hearing a point of view that most often paints an unrealistic picture of the story and the people involved. You're not being fair to the people involved by believing what is said about them.

Everyone has a point of view, and no one's life gets better by being unfairly judged—or by judging. You lower your vibrations when you gossip or listen to gossip. Politely turn away or change the subject, and people will stop bothering to gossip to you.

It's also none of your business what other people think of you. Don't worry about it! Wondering about what others think only makes you behave in a different way than you naturally would. That's no good! Besides, people don't think the way you think they think. They have their own thoughts!

Rather than finding your identity in what other people think of you, find your identity in your soul. We should be unique, and all people trying to conform to what social groups expect makes us all collectively and individually boring with a capital *B*. You don't need anyone else's approval to be happy. Value the opinion of the spirits who love you the most.

You can seek direct spiritual guidance from gurus. Teachers in school teach whether you want them to or not. Gurus are spiritual teachers who teach if, when and how you're ready to learn. Gurus help guide you toward your own spirit to find your spiritual self.

You probably have many gurus if you're on a spiritual path. You might come across some of them on purpose, like a person who makes a career out of helping people spiritually, and you might come across others completely out of the blue. You won't know ahead of time whether a person will be a guru for you or not.

You will find your gurus naturally if you set the intention to learn spiritually from the people you meet. You might:

- set out to have discussions with people you meet
- take a community class where you find someone who inspires you
- attend a spiritual yoga class
- attend a meditation retreat

- go to a seminar
- talk to a person who sees spirits and can help you with yours
- seek out a medium
- seek out a spiritual leader or shaman

Your one best and truest guru is you, and a really good guru will point you back to you. You have what you need to be happy and healthy inside of you. You don't always know what it is or how to find it, and it sometimes takes someone else pointing you there.

Since you are your own best guru, train your brain to act like a friend to you. Be your own best friend. Be nice to yourself. Stop the negativity. Treat yourself like you would treat someone you love.

No matter how lonely your human self feels, you can remember how loved you are by the divine charge. Remembering this will help your heart feel full. You can count on them! They've been waiting patiently your entire life to be able to help you more than they already do.

Playtime!
Dancing with the Divine

Describe the gaggle of divine charges that you talk to or would like to talk to. Add to it as you meet more. Look some up to meet even more.

Never Alone Unless You Want to Be!

Draw the ways you wish angels would help your friends, your family, and you right now.

Groovy Gurus

Be your own guru! Get into the habit of treating the kid in you like a child who is cared for and nurtured. Kids need adults in their lives. Well, once you become an adult, you *are* the adult in your life.

How about asking yourself some questions? (Thanks, Yogi Troy, for giving us the opportunity to do a project like this!)

You should really sit down to write the answers. A notebook that you can keep private from others is the best idea so that you can free write honestly. You can burn it later if you want, but it's really helpful to be able to read it in the future. When I wrote mine, I felt exposed when all the emotions came to the surface. When I reread it years later, after all those life situations had come to their own conclusions, I realized that I was again feeling the same way, but about completely different situations. It made me realize that worrying too much doesn't do any good.

When you see it in your own words and in hindsight, you see it so much more clearly.

If you want to share your words, even better! When you speak your own words aloud to another person, you learn your own feelings more than anything.

Help yourself slow down your thoughts by writing the answers to the questions that the adult in you asks the kid in you. It's like you are a parent to yourself asking the child in you questions.

The adult in you asks: How are you truly feeling right now?
The kid in you answers:

_____

_____

_____

_____

The adult in you asks: What fears are you feeling?
The kid in you answers:

_____

_____

_____

_____

_____

The adult in you asks: What are you like in your heart?
The kid in you answers:

_____

_____

_____

_____

_____

The adult in you asks: What are you like in your soul?
The kid in you answers:

_____

_____

_____

_____

_____

The adult in you asks: Do you feel that your spirit is light or like a weight is bearing down on it? Explain it to me.
The kid in you answers:

_____

_____

_____

_____

_____

The adult in you asks: In what ways are you honest with yourself?
The kid in you answers:

_____

_____

_____

_____

_____

The adult in you asks: Write about a time you were proud of yourself.
The kid in you answers:

_____

_____

_____

_____

The adult in you asks: Think about a time you succeeded at something. How did you feel?
The kid in you answers:

_____

_____

_____

_____

_____

The adult in you asks: What, if anything, would you like to change about your work life?
The kid in you answers:

_____

_____

_____

_____

_____

The adult in you asks: What, if anything, would you like to change about your love life?
The kid in you answers:

_____

_____

_____

The adult in you asks: What, if anything, would you like to change about your social life?
The kid in you answers:

_____

_____

_____

_____

_____

The adult in you asks: What, if anything, would you like to change about your financial situation?
The kid in you answers:

_____

_____

_____

_____

_____

The adult in you asks: Who *are* you?
The kid in you answers:

_____

_____

_____

_____

The adult in you asks: What are characteristics you dislike in other people?
The kid in you answers:

_____

_____

_____

_____

_____

The adult in you asks: Choose one of those characteristics. How can you be less that way yourself?
The kid in you answers:

_____

_____

_____

_____

_____

The adult in you asks: What characteristics do you admire in other people?
The kid in you answers:

_____

_____

_____

_____

The adult in you asks: Choose one of those characteristics. How can you be more that way yourself?
The kid in you answers:

_____

_____

_____

_____

_____

The adult in you asks: What do you like about yourself? Be thorough.
The kid in you answers:

_____

_____

_____

_____

_____

_____

_____

_____

_____

_____

Death, Suicide, and Our Real Home

With all the changes we go through in life, you might think we'd be used to the fact that nothing is permanent and we wouldn't be so shocked by death. We are shocked though, which is normal, especially when a loved one has died.

A lot of people die from illness or disease, and many people die earlier in life than expected. When this happens, the person's soul had previously planned the disease and early physical death on purpose. Why would they do that?

Because learning and helping us learn is the point of life on earth. How are we supposed to learn about the true nature of our spirituality if nothing bad ever happens? It might have been planned to help the research of medicine on earth, to help us learn lessons of a spiritual nature such as forgiveness, or to help activate awareness of some sort.

When a person suffers a traumatic death, the soul goes up from the body before the impact. The person who's set to die doesn't feel the pain unless the pain is meant to teach us something.

Many people commit suicide. In those instances, the soul had planned extreme life problems to advance as quickly as possible on the soul level. Unfortunately, their physical selves became overwhelmed, and they chose to end their lives early. They get back to heaven only to find their soul still wants to achieve the tasks. They'll often come back to the earthly plane with the same types of situations they previously had, but they have to start back at the beginning of life as newborns.

If you contemplate committing suicide, know that it took a lot of courage to take on this much pain and misery in your life. Be thankful that you've already gotten through as much as you have.

How old are you? If you're twenty-three, you've already succeeded at twenty-three years. Congratulations! You need to carry on from age twenty-three until your natural exit point, or you'll be starting all over again as a newborn and have to redo your situations through every age until you've made it all the way through.

Take pride in your courage for choosing such a difficult life path. Try to keep your head up and learn as much as you can while you're here just by being your own true self.

After you've lost someone close to you, you grieve the person's life as well as the life you had envisioned with that person. It probably leaves you wondering about the meaning of life. After someone you love dies, you might find it really tough to be happy. It's like the light inside of you has gone out. You walk through life just going through the motions—if that.

You're allowed to grieve! In fact, grieving helps you a lot more than hiding your feelings or pushing them aside or deeper inside you. It's not a good feeling, but let yourself feel the depression and rage. Be sad. Be mad at God. Notice your attachments. Maybe write down your thoughts and questions. Go through the motions of your daily routine without being mindful for a while.

Talk to a therapist. Talking helps because a person can give you advice, and when you talk to another person, you can clearly hear what you think and feel. When you keep it bottled up inside, it gets all jumbled and feels like it's taking over. When you say it aloud with words for another person to understand, you hear yourself in a different way.

Common, normal steps of grief are shock, denial, anger, bargaining, depression, testing and acceptance. Don't berate yourself for having those feelings! It's what happens when someone you care about is taken away from you.

You can help yourself. You know what to do and what not to do. If you allow yourself to heal, you'll know when it's time to move on. You will know when it's time to bring that light back and let it shine again. Only you can decide. There's no rule for how long it should take, but you owe it to yourself to try to get there sooner rather than later. Just try your best. That's all you can do.

There's no need to feel bad about things you didn't say to your loved ones while they were alive, such as, "I love you," "I'm sorry," or "goodbye." If you left each other on a negative note, feel comfort in the fact that there is no more negativity for a soul after death. After they die, they are all love, forgiveness and understanding.

If it helps to find closure, just say your words aloud. They can hear you!

Now that we know why people die, let's talk about what happens when the whole earth as we know it ends. Armageddon! Just joking. Actually, the world won't end in a scary way. Our spirits will go back to heaven, and we won't have to live on earth anymore. We won't need our low-vibration physical bodies or any of the other negativity we deal with on earth.

We aren't physical beings trying to be spiritual as much as we are spiritual beings in physical bodies. While we're here, let's do what we came to do. Let's raise our vibrations!

On that point, let's talk more about the good stuff. More and more instances are validating that heaven is beyond a white light we see when we die. Have you heard about a tunnel of light that you see when you die and go through to get to heaven?

A tunnel takes you to the other side, but it doesn't come down from the sky. It rises up from the etheric substance of your own body. The etheric substance, or ether, is the element that fills the part of our bodies that is most strongly connected to the spiritual world, and it fills the regions of space beyond earth's atmosphere.

The tunnel leads your spirit beyond a sort of veil where the vibrations are high. After physical death, you are pure spirit. You don't have a heavy body to weigh you down anymore, and you match those high vibrations and tune right in. Doesn't that sound simple and peaceful?

When this happens, you know right away that everything is all right, including the people you left behind on earth. You have an inner knowing that you'll see them again soon. When I say soon, I mean soon as on heaven's terms, where there is no measure of time like we have here on earth. A lifetime on earth goes by in a flash on heaven's terms.

If you're at peace with your earth life when you die, you can start enjoying heaven right away. If you have things to sort out—maybe you regret some of your life choices or killed yourself or someone else intentionally—your soul goes into a space where you rehabilitate and get counseling.

You don't have to be afraid of death for any reason. As soon as you get there, you remember everything your soul has known all along while you were at too low of a vibration to see. It's an indescribably beautiful and real place. Imagine the brightest and deepest colors you've ever seen—and then imagine them all enhanced thousands of times. There's no pollution, and there are no troubles.

When you die on earth, your spirit friends are right there to greet you in heaven. They are so excited that you're home. All your loved ones on earth who passed away, your pets, and your spirit friends who weren't on earth with you are there.

After the greeting, you go to the hall of wisdom. Your guides lead you to a smooth white marble bench, and you watch the scanning machine. It lets you scan yourself carrying through all the events of your life on earth.

After a near-death experience, people say, "I saw my life flash before my eyes." That's because they've been to the scanning machine—however briefly.

You see every good thing you did and all of the not-so-good things, including every time you said hurtful words or turned your back when you could've lent a helping hand. While you're watching the machine, you remember the chart you had written out for your life and analyze how well you handled life on earth.

No one sits in judgment of you, except for you. You're tough on yourself because your soul wants to advance as much as possible. Also, you're looking with spiritual eyes, which means you see things clearly. Since there's no negativity or ego in heaven, your spiritual eyes are honest and don't make excuses. You can also see what the other people in your life were dealing with. You see them with a new sense of compassion.

If the thought of watching yourself in this new light makes you feel good, then keep living life the way you're living it. If it makes you feel uncomfortable or ashamed, you can make whatever changes you see fit.

When you're in the comforts of heaven, you can watch over and be with your loved ones you left behind on earth. Some of your loved ones who are still on earth might be able to see your spirit—just as I did in the dream I had about my friend after she died and I'd prayed that I could laugh with her again. It was like she was right there with me.

Some might not be able to see your spirit, however, just as I never saw any other passed loved ones as clearly as I saw her. A lot of times, a person will see a spirit but pass it off as imagination or a memory dream. As a spirit, though, you understand this.

As a spirit, if you want to, you can manipulate objects to try to get people's attention. Maybe you leave coins around the house, change the TV channel, turn appliances on or off, sit next to them on the couch, or move pictures of you to different spots so they know it's you.

My grandma told us before she died that she was going to leave us pennies if heaven was any good, and dimes if it was great. I said, "We're going to be finding quarters all over the place!" She just laughed, but directly after she died, we started finding quarters in the oddest places, including in her shoe.

As a spirit, you'll be able to look at the charts your loved ones wrote for their lives. You can see what they will go through throughout the rest of their lives and the reasons their life paths were chosen the way they were. This can help you understand them, and since you can also see how they're going to overcome their obstacles, it reassures you that they will be okay. It will also help you be able to help them as they continue to chug along on earth.

As it is right now, since you're most likely still alive, you might like to know that you don't have to worry about spirits watching you when you're naked or otherwise indisposed. They do not care to look at you naked since the physical body isn't of any point of interest to spirits. They can also sense your energy and are respectful of your chosen alone time.

If the natural energy you're giving off is sending out messages that you want to be alone, your spirit friends respect that and give you privacy. Usually they're around when you're thinking about them or missing them a lot because they just want to comfort you and let you know they're okay and that they're there for you.

If you want to invite them in, there are different ways you can do it. Visualize being with them while you're up and about, quiet the mind with meditation, and sleep on a regular basis. Running on empty leaves your mind cluttered, making it difficult for them to get through to you. Delving into work and ignoring your feelings are other barriers. Periodically turn off the TV, computer, and phone, be in the quiet, and notice how you feel as you imagine communicating with them.

Trust your experience as being real as long as it makes you feel good. If the experience makes you feel bad in any way, paranoia is likely causing the experience—not your loved one's communication. Loving spirits will always communicate in loving ways.

If you're interested in visiting a medium, after a loved one has passed is a good time to do it. Evidently, your loved ones who have passed hear bells when you're visiting a medium and commune around you to give signs about who they are and what they want you to know. Be open to whatever sign they might use.

Remember, it's all about vibrations. Spirit vibrations are high, yours are low, and a medium is a go-between for communication. You won't lose anything by trying. Just think of what you could gain! You'd have reassurance that the person you miss so much is having a blast and is very much with you. That's worth knowing! Spirits might also give you guidance.

I remember a communication I had with my grandma after she passed. It was a dream where I asked her to help me figure out what direction to take in my new career. I finally heard an answer and recognized her voice. She said, "Whatever's fun." That sounded like something she would say, and it felt really good to know she cared enough to visit me even though she was in such a glorious place. I took it as a real spiritual experience. I realized it was her way of telling me to follow my passions and think of feelings of fun as signs for what to do. So, when making decisions, I think, "Which one feels more fun?" What a way to live! Thanks, Gramma!

Do you see that there's nothing to fear about death? It's like there's no such thing as death. We are more fully alive, happier, and more fulfilled in heaven than we ever are on earth.

In your true home of heaven, you continue to learn and live and work. Since the work you do is your passion, you love it. You do it because you want to, and you can change your work as often as you like so you're never bored.

You keep being you. You have your same personality and the same likes and dislikes—without any of the negativity or ego. If you disagree with another soul, you are so in tune with your spirituality that you immediately understand the other point of view, and the disagreement dissipates just like that. Also, if you don't care for someone else's personality, you don't have to hang out with them.

In heaven, you are who you are in your true, pure nature, when you're at your happiest and most filled with love. It sounds great, doesn't it?

The ecology of the land in heaven sounds great, too. It's totally balanced and flawless, but other than that, it's kind of like earth. The weather is perpetually calm, clear, and seventy-eight degrees. It's not too hot. That temperature only feels too hot on earth if your body runs hot or if there's humidity.

We don't have to worry about snowstorms, tornadoes, or hurricanes, and heaven doesn't need interstates or anything like that because we move by projected thought.

The animal kingdom abounds, and since they don't have to eat each other, they all live in peace with the rest of us. You know how dinosaurs died on earth? Well, they are still in heaven!

Heaven has the continents, mountains, oceans, rivers, deserts, forests, lakes, fields, islands, trees, plants, and every other part of the majestic landscape of nature. Since the landscape hasn't been ruined, it still has places that are lost to us on earth. Atlantis and LeMuria, which are continents lost to us in the Atlantic and Pacific Oceans, are still there. Also, the great libraries of Alexandria, which were destroyed by fire on earth, and the Dead Sea Scrolls look as good as new and are in perfect form. Greco-Roman style of architecture is used for the halls and temples we hang out in.

The scanning machine that shows you your earthly life is in the hall of wisdom. The location of the hall of wisdom corresponds to the West Coast of North America. Do you think it's more than coincidental that the West Coast is where so many spiritual healers and researchers reside?

Next to the hall of wisdom is the hall of records, which is one of the most popular buildings there. It is so full that there are also a lot of libraries for the overflow. They contain every passage that was ever published here on earth. There are books being written there that will be infused into human writers on earth so the information can be shared with the rest of us.

Also, the Akashic records contain every detail of every life on earth. On the other side of the hall of wisdom is the hall of justice where guides help us. There is also a statue of Azna, who is our mother god who heals us emotionally and physically.

The towers are structures that souls visit for the view, for meditation, and to receive counseling for any psychological or emotional issues after returning home from a life on earth. There are miles and miles of gardens containing every flower, stream and waterfall. You can sit and meditate under private flower canopies.

The hall of tones is a place you can visit to hum your personal mantras.

The hall of voices is where you can hear angels singing songs of worship.

There's a building of artwork, and a temple of lectures where you can learn public speaking and pretty much anything else you can imagine.

We don't need personal houses, but we can have them if we want them—and many spirits do. No matter how high your vibrations are, alone time is good if you like to be alone. Your house can look however you want it to, be wherever you want it, and move locations or change looks whenever you'd like. You create your home by projected thought, which is a concept we are just beginning to fathom on earth. There's no need to actually build homes, but there are builders who enjoy creating and building and spend time in heaven doing just that.

You choose how you work and play. Although there's no need for food, you can cook and eat if it's something you like to do. We don't need sleep, but we can lie down and rest whenever we want. There is no money, but don't worry, because there's no need for it. There's also no need to go to the bathroom!

There are fields where you can play whatever sports you like. You can surf or enjoy the snow that's there for you if you like.

You can take part in any creative art you choose. Can you guess what the answer is to the question of whether or not you're talented there? The answer is a loud, confident *yes*! We have limits here on earth that we simply don't have there.

We have parties with our friends. You can pick a few close friends or join a big group and dance and laugh and have picnics and festivals. You don't feel the desire to drink alcohol or do drugs because you're already happier and more content than you can imagine. There's just no reason to alter your mood.

We're all unconditionally accepted there. One of the reasons people go along with fads on earth is because we miss being so unconditionally accepted. It's a way to try to fill the void. We're never lonely in heaven. Plan to enjoy it. It's paradise—why wouldn't you enjoy it?

When your earth body dies and you go to heaven, you're not entering a place you've never been. You're getting back to a happy, busy life that you left behind for what will feel by then like a quick flash of time.

When you get there, what places will you visit? How will you live? Will you be close to the ocean, heavenly trees, plants and flowers? What will the people you hang around with be like? Will they be kind, happy and funny? Will you sing? Will you make inventions? Will you be funnier so you can do stand-up comedy and entertain the crowds? Will you listen to me while I attempt to? You don't have to because it's *your* heaven. Spend time daydreaming about your piece of heaven.

Heaven is an amazing place of growing and learning, although we learn at a much slower pace than we do here because everything is so easy and full of love there. We learn faster here because of the harsh environment, which is why we wanted to come here in the first place.

Do you wonder why there are schools and research centers there? Why would we need to keep learning? We don't need to. We want to! Only the highest being is all-knowing, but there's no limit to the amount of knowledge we can have, and our souls are curious to keep learning. We might not feel like that here, but that's only because our low vibration level weighs us down and stresses us out.

If you ever have feelings of worthlessness or of not fulfilling your purpose, those feelings are likely coming from your skills being limited here purposefully and for good reason. Just do your best with what you've got, appreciate it, and be proud of yourself for all the talents you do have— no matter how insignificant they might seem to you.

Another good reason to continue learning there is to benefit humankind and the universe as a whole. As spirits, we can share what we learn by infusing knowledge to the people on earth.

Since you're still an earthling, isn't that a great reason to meditate and follow your intuition? Some spirit might be trying to infuse knowledge that will lead to huge breakthroughs. You never know until you give it a chance.

No matter what you do, when your body is done being on this earth, you'll be glad this experiment is over. You'll be so proud of yourself for overcoming so many difficult situations. You'll be proud of yourself for all the good you did while you were here, and your soul will be obviously advanced as compared to before you left home to come here.

No matter what struggles you go through in life on earth—and it will be really difficult at times and keep changing, so you'll have different tough times at different parts of your life—it'll all be okay. Really! And then … it gets *so* much better!

Playtime!
Death, You Don't Have to Be So Scary!

How could you honor someone you love that has died? Do you think the person who loved you and passed away would want you to be sad or happy? Consider living the way they'd want you to live.

Can you imagine a life where you can remember your loved ones who have passed away, talk to them in your heart, and be happy all at the same time? Try it!

The Fun Times Stick Around—Only the Bad Times Are Gone!

Quickly list things that make you unhappy.

_____

_____

_____

_____

_____

_____

List things that make you happy.

_____

_____

_____

_____

_____

_____

Imagine a heaven where you automatically let go of all the unhappy stuff while holding on to all the things that make you happy.

Vibin' Earth Journeys

If you'd like to read parts of my story, you can decipher for yourself where I was pushing through doors that weren't going to open for me, and where doors opened for me so seemingly obviously. If you'd like to skip over the part about me, and get back to you, skip forward to the section entitled "Your Vibin' Journey."

My hope is that you'll be able to see the benefits of recognizing the doors that are meant for you rather than pushing yourself stressfully into places or situations that aren't truly right for you.

During seventh grade, I looked into the future and wondered what I wanted to do with it. I thought it would be best to be in a *place* I liked. I liked being at school, and I really liked being at home, so I decided I wanted to be a stay-at-home mom, and until that happened, I'd teach middle school.

A lot of doors opened for me. I was able to go to a good school and get an internship. After I graduated, I worked at two wonderful schools and taught awesome middle school kids. It was sure a lot of fun considering it was work!

After eight years, I was pushed out of what I loved and into a teaching position that I liked. I had tried to stop it from happening, but it was a lost cause. After five years of that, I pushed myself into a different teaching position that I thought I would love, and it turned into the most stressful two years of my life.

I thought back to when I had decided to be a teacher in the first place and how I had wanted to enjoy the place I was in. Well, I dreaded going there every day. My positive attitude took hours to build, and it was crushed within the first few minutes of the day—every day.

I started daydreaming about running away to Hawaii and doing yoga. What a dream! I loved that dream. I loved the running away part. I loved the Hawaii part, and I loved the yoga part. I desperately yearned to be in a place filled with happy people!

I kept up the daydream, but that was all it was—a daydream. I didn't plan to actually do anything about it. I had to keep my job; I had bills and responsibilities.

I prayed for better days, but that didn't seem to work. I said, in my prayers, that if I had a better day, I would stay put being a teacher. Whenever I prayed that prayer, I'm not kidding you, my day would be worse than when I didn't pray at all!

The people at the blood donation center said I couldn't donate anymore because of my emergency high blood pressure. For a short time I sort of had a classroom helper, but instead of helping, she would laugh telling me that she could see the color in my face changing when my blood pressure was going up!

The signs were notifying me to get out. In hindsight, it's apparent that my prayers were being answered the whole time—just not how I wanted them to be. I sure didn't know it at the time!

It took a while, but one day, I prayed, "Fine, God. I get it!" Yes, in my prayers, I yelled at the one who deserves the utmost respect, but I was so frustrated! I realized I was being asked: "How many times do you want me to tell you to get out?"

I had no plan B as far as careers go. What can you do with a teaching degree besides teach? It took a lot of courage to change my prayer, but eventually, I said that if I had a better day, I would quit teaching after the school year was over.

Guess what would happen? I would have a better day! Coincidence? I think not. I thought so at the time, so I tried it again and again. It was a good day each time.

I played with it. If I used my original prayer again, I would have a worse day. Finally, I got through the end of the school year promising to leave if it was a good day.

What could I possibly do next? I spent most of my time being stressed and wracking my brain about what my new career should be.

My daydream of running to Hawaii and teaching yoga never went away. I looked up yoga certifications, and the only one I saw that could get me certified before the next school year was in Chicago. I planned to sign up for it, but I never actually did. It just stayed on my to-do list.

I don't enjoy sitting at the computer, but that's how I searched seemingly endlessly for new job possibilities. Finally, one day I was on for only about three minutes and stumbled upon Peak Beings yoga certification in Hawaii during the month of July. What a dream come true!

I had a mortgage and a dog to take care of, so I didn't see it as a reality, until I talked to my family. They said they'd take my dog, take care of my yard work, and even send my bills if I left signed checks. They added, "You better hurry! Spots might fill up fast!"

I felt like I was floating so happily. It was my sign that I was on the right track.

I signed up right away and received a very quick, happy email from the teacher—with exclamation points and everything. I could practically hear him smiling over the email. That was another sign that I was on the right track. It had been so long since I had been surrounded by smiles that were happy rather than devious.

I suddenly knew that everything would be okay. I decided to let myself take the load off my shoulders and just enjoy my last month before the trip without worrying about the future. It felt so good to stop worrying. I thought, *It's yoga. We'll meditate, and I can figure it out then.* I didn't know how to meditate, but I knew they'd teach us.

I'm so happy that I followed through the doors that the universe was holding open for me. Otherwise, I might still be crying and praying out of frustration and maybe even have had a heart attack!

Running away to Hawaii was a total dream come true. What a life! Hawaii, it turned out, turned my future career options into holistic health. I doubt that studying in Chicago would have done the same.

One of the first things I did on the Big Island of Hawaii was go on a tour of the jungle. There are so many amazing plants, flowers and trees. The noni tree intrigued me the most. The tour guide described it as a healer. He said if we tied the leaves around our sore calves with a long sock, the pain would be gone by morning.

Guess what? He was right! My roommate and I are living testimonies. Unfortunately, the rest of my body was still sore, but that turned out to be a good thing, because that's how I got the idea to learn more about natural healing. I wanted to sleep in a noni tree!

Another plant we saw actually curls itself to protect itself when touched by human hands. After about four minutes, it opens back up. I felt like it was alive. When a ripe pineapple fell as we walked by, we opened it up and ate it. Doesn't the thought of living like that sound awesome?

I didn't want to have a roommate, but once I finally met her, all we needed were a few minutes before we knew we were going to have a blast. We'd laugh and laugh—just like I'd been missing for so long.

The yoga part of the day was great, too. We practiced for two hours each morning, and then we had the best breakfast buffet ever: granola, yogurt, organic peanut butter, fruit, and more. After a break, we learned about yoga for three hours while we sprawled out on the floor surrounded by jungle views and sounds.

Next would be an amazing lunch buffet and some free time. We'd usually go to the black sand beach, the pool or hot tub, take another nature hike, or join whatever classes were being offered in the area, such as weaving bracelets out of tree bark.

Later in the afternoon, we'd have another couple hours of class listening and learning from the book, followed by a buffet dinner. They cooked the island's own wild hogs and served the hands-down best bacon I'd ever tasted.

We had a bit more free time before bed. We'd often go for a walk or to the pool. Once, we went to watch an aerial show with people hanging from the ceiling and flipping around in hula-hoops. Little did I know that I'd be teaching aerial yoga in my future!

Some of my favorite memories of Hawaii are how genuinely nice everybody was. I think it's because they're so happy and so much less stressed by the daily grind. The daily grind usually includes doing things they love and plenty of sunshine and warmth.

One evening, a few of us took the resort's shuttle to the farmer's market. I was expecting vegetables and just the fun of being outside in Hawaii. Instead, I got a party! There was a band with dancing, homemade bracelets and other crafts, food and drink, and more laughter in a party atmosphere.

At one point, we went to the black sand beach and saw a naked yogi doing a headstand and then hanging upside down from a tree. We also found a coconut, broke it open, and drank out of it. On other days, we visited a waterfall and a volcano park and went on a hike to see the active volcanoes. At the end of our first week, our teacher told us people were complaining because we were laughing too loudly in the morning.

I was so grateful that our biggest problem was that we were too happy on our way to class before the sun even came up. I was there because I was running away from stressful situations with stressed-out people. I just wanted to be somewhere where people were happy, and I'd found it. I took it as a clear sign that I was in the right place and was headed in the right direction—even though I didn't know what that direction was.

I was thrilled that I was able to do all the yoga moves without much previous yoga experience. Pretty much everyone else had been to yoga studios, but I had not.

Our teacher led a lot of yogic breathing exercises. Now I realize how important and beneficial yogic breathing is. Now I even love to teach yogic breathing and meditation myself! That is not something I had ever even considered before.

Thanks to our teacher's consistency in having us practice various meditation techniques, I eventually had an amazing meditative experience. We had been doing a lot of sit-down meditations, and all I would think about was how uncomfortable I was and how much my knees hurt.

Then, we did a walking meditation. We had to walk so slowly—it could take a minute to take just a couple of steps—and I tried to imagine God walking next to me. As soon as it felt like he really was there, along came angels. I soon felt like I was being scooted or helped along. Next, my mom and dad and brother and everyone else I love were walking with me, too! I didn't feel like I was imagining it. Tears started forcing themselves down my face. I was walking toward a section of the room where I could see a jungle plant that looked like it was inside a door. I envisioned it as a door that the guy in charge of the world was opening for me to go through. It was the first time I'd ever thought about God's doors. I didn't know what would be on the other side of the door, but since everyone was still walking next to me, I continued on confidently.

As my meditation ended, I felt what it would be like to be successful in my next endeavor. I felt fluttery sensations in my chest. I felt what it would feel like to have helped people to have better lives, and I imagined the supreme being thanking me for helping him to help people through yoga and whatever else that door held for me.

I saw "Sleep in a Noni Tree" in my mind's eye. I thought it would be the name of my book about a journey from burned-out teacher to whatever came next. It served as a stepping-stone for this book. The meditation helped me sleep peacefully. I knew what my next steps in life would be: going through whatever doors the main dude of the universe opened for me.

After my next experience, I started wondering if I should stop telling these stories before people started thinking I was crazy.

A yogi was telling a story with teary eyes. I had read previously about sending thoughts of light. I remembered green light heals and white light protects, while other colors have certain benefits, too.

Without speaking or moving, I sent a bunch of colors into his chest, mainly green and white. I also asked Jesus to hug him and God to hold him in his hands now and whenever he needed it.

The storyteller stopped talking, wiped a tear, and said, "Wow. I just got a really strong sensation in my chest. Wow … that was weird. It felt really good. Okay." And then he moved on. You can call it a coincidence if you like, but I wouldn't buy it. It was purely spiritual, positive, healing and good!

The meditative experiences kept building in intensity as the month went on.

There was a Reiki practitioner in Hawaii. I like to call him Dan the Reiki Man. I didn't really understand what Reiki was, but I was excited for new experiences.

When I went to see him, I didn't have specific expectations, but my knee had been hurting and my muscles were sore. It had been a stressful couple of days trying to plan my first yoga routine to teach others, practicing it multiple times a day, taking the first classes others were teaching, and not being able to sleep. I had been anxious because I hadn't expected it to be so difficult to put a teaching routine together, and I was worried about what I would do with the rest of my life if I couldn't get through it smoothly. I hadn't officially resigned from my teaching position with the school district, and it was a very stressful thought that I might not be able to.

The Reiki man had stones for me to hold onto. He said they were for spiritual protection, unconditional love, self-healing, and something else, which I've forgotten. He asked if I had anything specific I'd like worked on. I told him that my knee hurt and asked him to help with whatever the chakras needed.

On the Reiki table, which is like a massage table, I was to focus on my breathing.

The Reiki man held a pendulum over my body, but I had my eyes closed and didn't see what he did with it or how it responded. He placed his hands on my shoulders, arms, wrists, knees, ankles, stomach and head. When his hands were at my head, I felt an itch on my nose. I decided to practice the yogi way of observing the sensation without becoming attached. Soon, the itch went away.

Then I heard a buzzing in my ear. I was going to have fun playing the game I'd called detachment, but I truly expected it to land on me at some point. The practitioner's hands were at my shoulders, so I thought he'd see it. Then I realized it wasn't leaving my ear—it would get louder and quieter, but it never left the ear area.

So, while on this Reiki table, in Hawaii, with a high-pitched sound buzzing in my ear, I realized I might be hearing my spirit guide talking to me. I silently told him that I could hear him. The buzzing quickly became louder and higher pitched. I really tried to concentrate. I didn't feel I had deciphered anything from it, but it was absolutely beautiful and uplifting to me. It disappeared soon, and soon after that, the Reiki man asked me to start coming back to my body.

I didn't want to! I resisted for a while, and I noticed that I couldn't tell whether my body felt very heavy or very light. It was a strange sensation. My left foot felt the strangest. It felt a bit like it was almost asleep, but it wasn't the same as after I had sat on my feet for too long. It felt like my body, especially my left leg, was directly on top of the rest of my body. The feeling reminded me of when people used bunny ears on the TV and the channel would go out, leaving the static sound with gray, black and white patterns jumping around on the screen.

I wiggled and got up, and my leg still felt different. When I hopped off the table, my knee didn't hurt at all! I could not remember the last time it had felt so free of pain. It was amazing.

The rest of me felt amazingly light, too. I told him that I didn't remember ever relaxing so quickly and that my body felt different. He said that was music to his ears.

He said my sacral, third eye, and crown were blocked. As sad and surprised as I was about the third eye, I was sadder about the crown. I felt like I'd been putting everything else aside to focus on a new career for more than a year, and since my crown was closed, I was essentially trying to do it by myself. No wonder I wasn't getting the clear answers I'd been hoping for!

Since that specific Reiki man listened to and trusted his intuition, he let me know that he kept getting the message during my treatment that I had to let go with humor. He said I'd been going hard for a long time, metaphorically and physically, and that I didn't know why it didn't seem to be getting me anywhere. If I let go with humor and kept my chakras open, the answers would start pouring in.

He said that adults think we need to control everything, plan everything out, and worry if we don't have the answers. He said that I had to let go, take care of myself spiritually and health-wise first and foremost and enjoy the perfect moment that is at each moment.

He suggested I massage my head and tap my third eye to keep me moving forward in balance with my health and wellbeing and letting go with humor. He suggested EFT, which is the emotional freedom technique. He also suggested meetup.com to find spiritual healing groups in my area. He suggested I find a Reiki Master in Wisconsin for a Level 1 Attunement so I could self-heal. I wonder if he knew he was practically handing me my new life path. I'm guessing he intuitively knew he was being guided to give me that specific information.

He also suggested that I journal, which I have been doing since I was young, and that *Letting Go* could be the name of my first book. I thought that was cool because I hadn't told him that I was planning on writing a book. I hadn't told him anything else about my life, either!

I mentioned the itch on my nose and the bug in my ear. He said that could be one of two things. I wanted to hear him say it! Instead, I got excited and spoke first. I said that maybe it was my spirit guide, and he said that's the one he was leaning toward. He hadn't seen any bug, plus we were in an enclosure, and there were no bugs in there.

He asked if I had noticed my breathing changing during the treatment. That was how he knew I had gone somewhere and it was his opportunity to work on my spirit alone, which is the best way to get results. He said I was really open to this process and leaving to the spiritual world, which was music to my ears.

I told him about my student who told me about my imaginary friend, Jason.

He asked if it was the first time I had heard the sound. I couldn't remember, but I told him about the time I had heard the big pop in my bedroom after meditating on my spirit guide. The pop is the sound spirits might make when entering or exiting the earthly realm.

I mentioned that I had gone to see a Sylvia Browne talk and how she had answered my question. He said he'd gone to see her once too, and she had also answered his question. It felt so wonderful to have that conversation, and I felt better than I had in a very long time.

I took pictures of the tarot cards he laid out and read for me, and would you believe that photo turned out more clearly than all of the other pictures I took? Those cards are the ones I mentioned in the tarot section.

At dinner practically everyone told me how great I looked, and they had spent the entire day with me, so this was in comparison. One friend commented that I was absolutely glowing. Most of them signed up for a Reiki appointment of their own for the next day.

I felt so amazing, so at peace, and so happy to just have fun and stop worrying.

For the rest of the night, I was walking on air and loving every minute. All the nervousness I'd had about teaching my first yoga class the following morning had completely vanished—and was replaced with pure joy and excitement for it.

I added some chakra meditation ideas into my lesson before I went to bed.

I also reflected on the things Dan the Reiki man had said spirit was telling him. I had to take care of myself, I should stop doing things according to what others wanted me to do, I should meditate light and colors on myself rather than always onto others and the world, and I should get in touch with my inner self.

I was too excited to sleep!

That Reiki experience was such an obvious expansion of the successful meditation I'd had about walking through whatever doors were open for me. I felt so excited to be in touch again with my spirits and to have my chakras open.

The intermittent sleep I got was plenty for the next day. I awoke feeling great and had no nervous energy, physical pain or worries.

I taught my first yoga class just fine.

When it was time to leave the island, my roommate gave me the going-away gift of my very own statue of Ganesh. She said a friend had given her one and amazing things came into her life. She gave one to everyone she loved and watched amazing things show up in their lives. She said it would bring me every happiness in my career and relationships. I didn't know who Ganesh was, so I had to look it up. I read the description aloud, and my roommate simply responded, "He's awesome!"

I was leaving Hawaii and at the threshold of my new career. I wanted to keep my focus on noticing doors that were opened for me rather than pushing through others, but that meant I had to keep my anxiety at bay and my chakras open. Trying not to be anxious made me anxious.

"God's doors" was my mantra.

The day I got home, I got a mass email from my fitness center about their monthly updates. I figured it was a no-reply email, but on a whim—or maybe because of my intuition—I took a chance and replied. I told them that I had just come home from Hawaii with my yoga certification and asked them to call me if they needed another yoga teacher.

The next day, they responded: "What days and evenings would you be free?" *Ding-dong!*

I would have at least one hour per week of work when I officially resigned from school. It might not sound like a very smart plan, but I was putting my faith in rolling with it and doing what felt right. In honor of keeping anxiety at bay while trying to plan for my future, I grabbed a tea bag, got down on my yoga mat, and held it over my chakra line, pausing over each and trying to notice the movements.

I was disappointed, but not surprised, that some of my energy levels already seemed low. I put my hands over my chakras and asked for healing energy. I actually felt better, and it was fun to feel as though I'd discovered something new about myself. I was new to it and wanted to know how to do it better, so I ordered the Reiki toolkit from the International Center for Reiki Training. I did some research on yoga studios and holistic health places in the area, and then I went for a walk to let go of my nagging thoughts.

On my walk, because I stopped trying so hard to think, think, think, the thoughts actually came to me. Great ideas were coming to me about what to add to my resume, and it was so uplifting to realize I actually had a lot of assets for a company about holistic health education. I had a yoga certification, a master's degree in education, a health minor, an interest in pursuing Reiki and any other holistic health certification, and was willing and able to travel.

On my second night home, I went to a fish fry with my parents and two friends. I told them about my experiences and desires to teach yoga, do Reiki, and maybe even have my own business.

When my dad asked what I would do next, it scared me to hear myself say, "I don't know." I felt so unprepared. I wanted the universe to lead me somewhere and tell me where to go—and for something to come along that just felt right—but I couldn't just sit around and wait. I really didn't know what step to take next. Singing "Ice Ice Baby" and "Humpty Dance" at karaoke got me through the evening.

The next morning, I was excited to prepare my cover letter and resume for the holistic education place I had found, but the website for the institute was disappointing to me. It was not what I had expected or hoped for at all. I went back to the drawing board and to the art of practicing letting go, but not without a few tears.

I decided to practice teaching yoga, so I held a free class at the beach. I advertised on social media, and people who live too far away responded that they would be there if they could, but very few people from home responded at all. Four people did show up—my parents and two friends. One friend partook while the others watched (my parents felt too old, and my other friend felt too pregnant). It was a confidence boost to practice teaching successfully, so it was well worth it.

On the way home, I thought I should see if there were any commercial properties for sale for a business of my own. A few seconds later, I saw one that seemed perfect. I was amazed and took lots of pictures. Then I realized that the reality of owning a business was more than I wanted to take on, so

I went to accomplish something easy. I picked up some ink for the printer. Next, I emailed some cover letters and resumes and hooked myself up to career-finder websites.

That night, I had a dream that I was traveling and noticed what I had packed. I decided to meditate on the meaning of it. I thought it meant that I had to figure out where I wanted to go and what I needed to get there, so I decided to finalize and print my portfolio pages to carry with me.

I realized I wanted to do holistic healing of all sorts for my new career. It may seem obvious, but it hadn't clicked for me yet. I was so excited. It had only been five days since I got home, and I knew what I wanted to do with my life!

The next day, I got a response from the owner of a yoga studio in the next town. I was so excited when I returned her call, but she reprimanded me for applying with a cover letter and a resume! Our teacher had talked about becoming a client first, but I needed a job soon! She schooled me on being a client first and getting to know her type of yoga. She asked what type of yoga I taught and gave me very opinionated views on how she only believes in her kind of yoga.

I felt like I'd missed an opportunity and dodged a bullet at the same time!

A friend who had listened to my Reiki story forwarded a notice about an actual Reiki Level 1 Attunement being offered in my area. I had not previously believed that I could find a teacher so close to home.

I was still barely home a week from Hawaii when I earned my certification, becoming a Reiki practitioner with plans for becoming a teacher of it as soon as I could.

It was the first really sunny, beautiful day since I'd been home, and I was more than happy to be inside, which isn't a normal feeling for me on a warm and sunny day. Being in the spot that was best for me was a terrific feeling after a week of stressing and worrying about where to work and how to get there. I didn't see it as being feasible as a full-time job any more than I could see yoga as being one, but I still felt great about it.

We did a muscle experiment in the beginning where we put our arms out and resisted each other pushing down on them. Our teacher, Sarah, simply split the air downward with her hand—like in Tae Kwon Do but without much force—and asked us to resist her push again. This time, our arms went down very easily. She had us refresh and resist normally again. It was easy to resist. She had us think of something sad, and when she pushed down again, our arms went down easily. That's how much power energy has! The thoughts we have affect our energy, and energy moves upward, which is why it broke the energy when she moved her hand down and when we made ourselves sad.

The actual attunement had us sitting in chairs with our eyes closed while our teacher did her thing. I felt energy like white light going down into my crown and through my body, down to my feet and back up again, but it didn't seem to leave my body. I tried to concentrate on certain thoughts to help it become stronger inside of me.

Sarah comforted me later, saying that I don't have to do anything to make this energy strong because it is guided spiritually and has a mind of its own. It comes from the higher dimension, the universe, or whatever higher power the person believes in. I love that because it takes the responsibility off of me, so I can be less anxious about doing it wrong. In fact, there is no wrong way because Reiki can never harm. It's pure love and healing energy coming from a source who wants us to heal.

She said that because of all the healing energy going through us in one day, there might be symptoms as the toxins left the body, which could come in the form of being sick. She said to do Reiki if it happened and to take a salt bath because salt is a magnet to draw out toxins. She said the bath water might even become dark.

I thought there was no way I was going to get sick. I felt great that evening, and I went to bed feeling awesome. However, in the wee hours of the morning, I had stuffy nostrils. Ten minutes later, I threw up! I took a salt bath, and ten or so minutes after that, I had a nasty number two. I fell asleep, and when I woke up a couple hours later, I felt very lethargic. I got out of bed and realized, very suddenly, that I felt better than I had all week. It was amazing! I saw the world in my favorite way; everything made me happy.

With how happy I felt, I remembered what Sarah had said when I mentioned that people would think I was weird for doing it. She had said, "Who cares? Let them. Once they realize how happy you are, they'll think, 'Hey, I wonder if there's something to that after all.'"

Since I was back at home, I was back on the job-finding mission. I'd applied to thirteen places, but only two of them were even hiring. I had my resume on multiple job-finding websites, all of which came to no fruition. When I did finally get a response, I realized that my resume made it look like I was keeping my full-time job! The ending date read *current* since I hadn't yet resigned.

Had I sabotaged my chances? To make success seem even further away, I wondered if I should go back to teaching. I applied to the technical college in town, only to find out that my master's degree in education plus forty-six credits wasn't enough to qualify me to teach there because I needed more specific credits!

I felt so defeated! But I still felt like resigning from my current job was the right thing to do—so I did it.

Directly after I resigned, a complete stranger asked me if I was feeling balanced. I knew with my whole being that I was! It turned out he had just been reading the front of my shirt, which said, "Balance," but still.

Within the next two weeks, I acquired two more jobs from the cover letter and resume; each was two hours per week. One was teaching yoga, and one was teaching yoga and other holistic topics of my choice. Whew! Still, even with three jobs, I was only at five hours per week. Luckily, I had Reiki appointments scheduled for family and friends. My parents were my most frequent clients, but that's an awesome way to start!

I spent time learning choreography to teach cardio dance, but I was only successful at memorizing forty minutes out of sixty, so that didn't go far.

I needed something to lean on. Even though I had never wanted to be a bartender, I spent my birthday earning my online beverage server certification. I only applied to one restaurant/bar, and they didn't take me, so that never became a job.

I put a lot of time and energy into creating a website, but I only got responses from scammers. I set up a special Reiki Facebook page, but I only received friend requests and likes from people I knew in high school who weren't even interested in Reiki. I set up a Facebook page called Noni Tree Healing in order to promote the services I wanted to offer, but it mostly got followers from people in other countries who were interested in noni trees and juice.

In September, I received my Reiki Level 2 certification. I was one step closer to becoming a teacher of it! I was so happy to be a yoga teacher, but pleasing everyone who comes to class is difficult—and trying to do so made me nervous. I got into the habit of asking Jesus to do yoga next to me while I was teaching and to guide my next moves. It helped so much! I would still find that some people didn't like the class, but a year later, I realized that not even Jesus pleased everyone, so I could stop trying.

It had been news to me when my yoga teacher in Hawaii had said these were the days of getting jobs because of people you know rather than by resumes. That's all fine and dandy if you know someone! Luckily, it turned out that I did. Eventually, I would meet more.

At the beginning of January, my cousin called looking for a part-time online employee to do content-review work. I'd be working from home and using my college education—score! The job, which came to me out of the blue, helped me feel less like a fish out of water and more like I had time to wait for holistic doors to open to me.

In February, some friends led schoolteachers to ask me to bring yoga to their students. That was fun!

In March, I earned my Reiki Master certification from William Lee Rand, and I could finally teach it, attune others to it, and certify people to be teachers.

I knew things were going well because of the little things that were becoming so much better. A picture fell right off the wall and didn't even freak me out. As luck would have it, it didn't even break.

In April, a friend's mom sent my first nonfamily member/non-friend Reiki client. I soon had handfuls of Reiki students who I had attuned to the Reiki energy.

I had sent a resume and cover letter to the yoga studio in town when I got home from Hawaii, but they hadn't responded to it. Little did I know someone I would meet would be the metaphorical door I needed. I met Sandy at a holistic health fair, entered her raffle, and won a free healing treatment (ding-dong on the free healing treatment door, too!)

When I went in for my treatment, Sandy and I got to know each other and she said that I was a natural healer. I was dumbfounded by how many people were telling me that! She said I had gold coming out of my fingertips and that I could just touch people and make a difference, but I had to put my energy into it and trust myself. She said Reiki could help, but I could do it just by putting my energy into it. She asked if I already knew that, and I said, "Yeah, sort of, but I always just thought it was my imagination."

She retorted, "Stop that!"

When I left the house, I felt like I was flying like a kite.

She hooked me up with the owners of the yoga studio in town. I got a job there subbing classes and then teaching my own yoga classes and holding workshops for Reiki, chakra healing, meditation, and breathing exercises. I even became certified for teaching aerial yoga.

A coworker led me to landing another permanent yoga teaching job in another facility.

Sandy introduced me to essential oils, and I ended up selling them as yet another part-time job. I'm not a good salesperson, but I truly enjoy learning and healing from the oils, and it's nice to have the availability to offer them to others.

Since I love hip hop and cardio, I was excited to have the opportunity to teach hip hop step, which would be fun but take a lot of time and practice. It didn't work out because the lady in charge misread one of my texts! That hip hop step door was bound to close on me soon, anyway.

My back began to hurt a lot. Nothing I did helped, and the doctor said I was fine. It hurt less when I sat. Luckily, I was expecting a writing project for my online job; that would keep my hyper self close to the couch.

The writing project never came! So, for months and months I would teach a couple yoga classes a day, then write this book while sitting on the couch in pain.

The week after I printed out the first final version of this book, I found the person who would be able to heal my pain! Thanks Tony, Chinese medicine, acupuncture and herbs!

Coincidence? I think not!

I'm naturally too hyper to sit long enough to write a book from start to finish. Just ask the other books I've written. Oh, you can't because they're not finished!

I had to find the doors that were being held open for me. It took a while, and it took a lot of courage to wait, but there were a lot of open doors. It was just a matter of letting go of the grips of time and control while turning onto the paths I was meant to take.

Here is my horoscope from 2013 when I taught my last semester of school and started my new career of holistic healing:

> Your relationship with the universe in the year ahead will be like that of the teacher's pet. Yes, Virgo, you will be blessed with abundance and many opportunities to find your true self and to be your best self. There will be lessons to learn, of course, but you will have amazing guidance toward your goals and almost mystical assistance with your dreams. All the universe requires is that you remain optimistic and that you accept the opportunities you are given. If you do, this will be a magical year for you.

It was from a free app called "Daily Horoscope." I never did any research on the validity of the writer, but it sure was fitting to me—yearly as well as daily.

If I had trusted that the things the horoscope said were true while I was living out the year, I would have had an easier time. I'm not saying that you should fully trust horoscopes, but trust yourself and your divine guidance. If it weren't for divine guidance, who knows where we'd be?

Your Vibin' Journey

You're never lost in life, but there will be times when you're meant to feel lost. It's all a way to help you figure out your path. It's okay to feel apprehensive during those times, but it's also a good idea to experiment, take risks, and even make mistakes.

Change is inevitable. You won't have to be stuck long even when your doors close. Don't restrict yourself to certain rules that will bring you down. Be patient!

Spending time with the divine is more productive than time spent metaphorically (or physically!) banging your head against a wall.

Practice getting in touch with your intuition. It's the smartest and quietest part of you. Meditate and jot down what works—and what doesn't—as you practice listening to it.

Power on getting to know your inner self!

Even though there are more levels of consciousness than can be counted, understanding four main levels that humans experience might help as you explore your spiritual path.

People in level 1 haven't realized that they're part of the divine. They live in fight-or-flight mode because life is a game of survival for them. There's a lot of fear in that game, and they tend to be defensive and focus on differences, pain and crime. When people don't let themselves feel spiritual energy, crazy things happen! We see a lot of crazy things happening—it's all over the news if not right in your own neighborhood. When people in level 1 mess with your life, try to forgive them. You don't have to actually tell them if you don't want to, but you still need to do it for your own healing. Visualize forgiving them and saying, "I forgive you." It takes time to let go after tragedy strikes, but forgiveness can help ease it along.

People in level 2 have stepped out of survival mode and are on some sort of a spiritual journey—whatever each person happens to call it. They have begun to let go of their egos. Rather than thinking about the self as the main priority, they see that we're meant to experience life together. They accept differences and know that differences help us grow. They're learning to feed themselves spiritually and are learning to love others for who they are spiritually.

People in level 3 are spiritually wise and influential. They set out to make sacrifices for the spirituality of others.

People in level 4 have entirely shed their personal egos. They completely understand that the whole universe is one, live as examples to the rest of the world, and dedicate their lives to helping others spiritually.

It's a gradual movement from one level to the next, and we tend to go back and forth even as we move forward.

Keep on noticing what spiritual stage you're in—and keep reaching for the next stage. You won't know what it will be until it is, but don't feel like you should be further along than you are.

We are all different, and we're meant to be that way. It shouldn't be surprising to learn that our spiritual journeys will all be very different. That's a good thing!

As you step along, don't be afraid to share your spiritual news with other people. We are in this together! Simply be an example of a shining spirit with high vibes and let other people match your vibes if they choose. Notice where you think a person is energetically and shed your light to raise their vibrations. Be like light with kindness, happiness, and love.

Considering what you know now about why we chose this life, how do you feel about judging others? Everyone should be allowed to be 100 percent who they are.

The best way to accomplish living your best life is by just being you! Isn't that great news? You might have to get to know yourself a bit better. Let go of society's expectations of you. Let go of society's expectations of others. Let others be who they are, and … just be you!

You're meant to extend *your* light, *your* love, and *your* vibes, and only you can do it the way *you* do it. Out of the mind, body and spirit, the spirit tends to get squished the most, but you can change that. You have the power to make your spirit vibrate higher—no matter what. When you get out of your head and live through your spirit and soul, you'll notice situations that used to seem so important beginning to seem silly and easier to manage. Think of your short interactions and reactions as perfect times to do your vibration experiments. Your vibes will be too high to be brought down, and little miracles will pop up around you like crazy.

Going forward, focus on the important things in life:

You rock—no matter what. Yes, I said *you*. You rock! Be you.

Have FUN with your experiments on this magical journey. Even when you lose a battle, you'll thrive on. Do things just because they're fun—and enjoy finding your playground! Be happy.

Stop hating! It's good to let go of all fear. You can let it all go to the spiritual world to dissipate.

Try to think of passing on from this life as a good thing—or at least in as much of a positive light as you can muster because heaven is our true home, and it is awesome! Going back is like the most amazing graduation present there could ever possibly be, and it's from the toughest school there will ever be.

Remember that your loved ones who have passed on from this life are happy. You can imagine all the fun they're having! They will always love you, and they're here with you whenever you want. It's good to take the time you need to grieve and express your feelings, but do your best to stop your negative thoughts because everything really is better than okay.

Trust your inner guidance, and you won't be led astray!

Playtime!
Go Get High on Vibes!

See yourself the way the divine charge sees you. You'll be so happy from the inside out! You'll be able to change the world with your vibrations, and you'll be making a lot of difference. Start from inside you, raise your vibes, and spread them around. Have fun watching the domino effect, and remember that it's all just another part of the vibration experiment!

Vibration Experiment Rap (A Fun Mantra)

It's all a big experiment
within my soul.
I play on my path—
That is the goal.

I trust my inner guidance,
I won't be led astray.
I don't know my path yet—
But, see ... that's okay!

I play with my spirit,
I play with my vibes.
Check in with the universe—
It's what it prescribes.

It's all a big experiment,
Yes, life is.
I play with vibin' higher
To heal my biz.

I heal my mind,
And heal my bod.
It's in my spirit
Where I find my god.

Hope in my heart,
But fear in my head?
I focus on my heart—
Forget that dread!

It's all a big experiment,
Yes, life is.
I play on my journey—
It is what it is!

Printed in the United States
By Bookmasters